The Greatest Thing in the World

Henry Drummond's

The Greatest Thing in the World

The Restored Gospel Version

The Greatest Thing in the World

Other Books by Bill Wylson

Hieroglyphs, Golden Plates & Typos
Give Place in Your Heart
Three Minutes Eighteen Seconds
Elder Hammond and The Inspector
The Manger on the Mantle
A New Earth

Books Available in Spanish:

Tres Minutos con Dieciocho Segundos

Henry Drummond's

The Greatest Thing in the World

The Restored Gospel Version

Bill Wylson

The Greatest Thing in the World

Green Stem Press
Copyright © 2020

All rights reserved. Except as permitted under the United States Copyright Act of 1976, and in the case of brief quotations embodied in reviews, no part of this publication may be copied, reproduced or distributed in any form or by any means, or stored in a database or retrieval system, without the prior written authorization from the author.

ISBN-13: 978-1-7342387-2-3
ISBN-10: 1-7342387-2-0

Text from:
The Greatest Thing in the World and Other Addresses, by Henry Drummond:
The Project Gutenberg: for the use of anyone anywhere at no cost and with almost no restrictions whatsoever. You may copy it, give it away or re-use it under the terms of the Project Gutenberg

www.gutenberg.net
Release Date: September 24, 2005

Produced by David Garcia, Jeannie Howse and the Online Distributed Proofreading Team at
http://www.pgdp.net

Green Stem Press
A White Horse Book

greenstempress.com
myldsbooks.com

The Greatest Thing in the World

Publisher's Note:

Get More Out of This Book

Sterling Sill, author of over 30 books, once wrote about an article he read entitled *How to Get More Out of a Book Than There Is in It.* "Good readers," he explained, "may be able to get out of a book all there is in the book, but with a little imagination and some ability to analyze, they may get much more."

All capable readers can have their thoughts strike a particular notion, causing their thinking to drift away from the material they are reading. We should not be too quick to draw our minds back into the book, since frequently if we give our imagination a little freedom, it will direct us to some interrelated way of thinking that could prove to be extremely valuable.

People may often find that the most significant insights, ideas and beliefs are the ones that they come up with on their own and not so much from the concepts printed on the page. As our mind wanders along its own specific chain of correlated thought, we may arrive all on our own at some important interpretations and impressive conclusions. Then, when our minds have finished their journey of exploration and discovery, we can return our attention to the book and resume reading.

This is how to get more out of a book than there is in it. The book will cause us to come to conclusions regarding a diversity of notions not actually in the book. The interest of freeing our thoughts is an extremely beneficial and rewarding undertaking.

Paul, the New Testament apostle, was a known ponderer. He advises us that "whatsoever things are true, whatsoever things are honest, whatsoever things are just, whatsoever things are pure, whatsoever things are lovely, whatsoever things are of good report . . . think on these things." The ability to ponder gives us the capacity to obtain more from our circumstances and situations than what is actually in them. Through this procedure we place ourselves above the conventional and commonplace existence.

Thousands of fantastic, fascinating philosophies are frittering away in countless books. Hundreds of important and profound programs that could benefit us immensely sit untouched on library shelves. Even the word of God Himself remains largely unfamiliar and unacquainted to many of us. All the essential

The Greatest Thing in the World

ingredients for success in any of our personal pursuits cannot advance our progression until we ingest and absorb them; until we get them circulating in our bloodstream and make them a part of our inner strength and learning.

As you read this book, or any other, practice the art of pondering. It will give you a more prolific passion for learning and thinking and, hopefully, for putting into practice. If what you read here does not please and persuade you, so much the better. You can amend each page or each chapter to your own specific situation to satisfy your own particular prerequisites.

Effective pondering will enable you to draw concrete conclusions and form compelling objectives on the vital subject of your personal progress in life.

The Greatest Thing in the World

"TO BE JUSTIFIED BEFORE GOD WE MUST LOVE ONE ANOTHER."

JOSEPH SMITH, JR.

The Greatest Thing in the World

To my beautiful wife, Connie.

I cannot read 1st Corinthians 13, Moroni 7, or Henry Drummond's The Greatest Thing in the World without seeing the selfless, loving image of my sweet wife reflected in every attribute, every quality, and every characteristic of charity, the pure love of Christ.

The Greatest Thing in the World

Disclaimer:

Author's Note: Some of the ideas discussed in this work relate to doctrines and teachings of the Church of Jesus Christ of Latter-day Saints. However, the ideas expressed herein represent nothing more than the opinion of the author. I have no authority or commission to speak in any official capacity for the Church.

Henry Drummond's original text from "The Greatest Thing in the World" is copied herein in italics.

The Greatest Thing in the World

Table of Contents

Introduction   15

The Greatest Thing in the World   19

The Contrast   39

The Analysis   61

The Defense   121

Drummond's Original Text   143

About the Author   189

Other Books by Bill Wylson   191

The Greatest Thing in the World

"LOVE IS ONE OF THE CHIEF CHARACTERISTICS OF DEITY, AND OUGHT TO BE MANIFESTED BY THOSE WHO ASPIRE TO BE THE SONS OF GOD. A MAN FILLED WITH THE LOVE OF GOD, IS NOT CONTENT WITH BLESSING HIS FAMILY ALONE, BUT RANGES THROUGH THE WHOLE WORLD, ANXIOUS TO BLESS THE WHOLE HUMAN RACE."

JOSEPH SMITH, JR.

INTRODUCTION

Among the precious treasures my father left me after he passed away was *The Greatest Thing in the World*—or, more precisely, a worn and tattered copy of Henry Drummond's beloved little book. On the inside cover my father had written a goal for himself:

"Read once every month."

The Greatest Thing in the World

Obviously, he had some difficulty achieving that goal.

Regardless, the book's broken binding, the tattered and torn pages and the numerous annotations and passages underlined in red pencil indicate that my father studied the book extensively.

When I first read *The Greatest Thing in the World,* I made a similar goal to study the little book once every month. My initial results mirrored my father's. But as I began to gain a greater understanding of the *summon bonum* and the pivotal position of the wonderous gift of charity, I began to make notes and comparisons with modern-day scripture and writings.

As I did so, it became clearer to me why Mr. Drummond, the apostle Paul and the ancient American prophet Mormon all refer to the supreme gift of charity as the "greatest of all." My objective in writing this book is to share with you the meaningful words of Henry Drummond's marvelous exposition with the added perspective of modern revelation.

In this book, Henry Drummond's original text appears in italics.

I will leave it up to you how many times you wish to read the book.

The Greatest Thing in the World

"Life has its share of fears and failures. Sometimes things fall short. Sometimes people fail us, or economies or businesses or governments fail us. But one thing in time or eternity does *not* fail us—the pure love of Christ."

Jeffry R. Holland

Chapter One

THE GREATEST THING IN THE WORLD

Has Christianity missed the mark?

Everyone has asked himself or herself the great question of antiquity as of the modern world: What is the summum bonum—the supreme good? You have life before you. Once only you can live it. What is the noblest object of desire, the supreme gift to covet?

We have been accustomed to be told that the greatest thing in the religious world is Faith.... If we have been told that, we may miss the mark.

The word faith appears around 260 times in the Book of Mormon and, depending on the translation, anywhere from 336 to 521 times in the Bible. We are told that through faith in Christ we enter into grace, are forgiven, cleansed, sanctified, saved, raised up, made alive, born again, transferred from darkness to light, made righteous, justified, become sons and daughters in Christ, given the Holy Spirit, accepted by God, and have eternal life. [1]

The foundation for all of our spiritual growth is faith. Elder M. Russell Ballard tells us that "faith in the Lord Jesus Christ is the main anchor we must have in our lives to hold us fast during times of social turbulence and wickedness that seemed to be everywhere today." [2]

Additionally, we are told that faith, through the power of the Holy Spirit, can reveal truths, change hearts, remit sins, and sanctify. [3]

---

[1] Acts 11:17, 15:7-9,16:30-31, 26:18, Romans 3:21-26, Galatians 3:21-26.
[2] Ballard, M. Russell, *Anchor Your Soul*, The New Era March 1993.
[3] Jarom 1:4, Mosiah 4:3, 5:4-7, Alma 9:20, 3 Nephi 27:19.

Through faith miracles are manifest. [4]
Angels appear. [5]
Mountains are moved. [6]
Battles are won. [7]
Prison walls crumble. [8]

The Law was given to Moses by faith and by faith Christ appeared to the inhabitants of the ancient Americas. [9]

Great faith has permitted certain individuals to see Christ and to have all things revealed to them. [10] We are told that the Savior "claimeth all those who have faith in him; and they who have faith in him will cleave unto every good thing." [11]

It is through our faith that he grants us eternal life. [12]

We are reminded several times that "the Lord is able to do all things according to his will, for the children of men, if it so be that they exercise faith in him." [13]

---

[4] Ether 12:16,18.
[5] Moroni 7:30.
[6] Jacob 4:6, Mormon 8:24, Ether 12:30
[7] Alma 57:21.
[8] Ether 12:13.
[9] Ether 12:1, 7.
[10] Ether 3:9, 4:7, 12:8-31.
[11] Moroni 7:28.
[12] Helaman 8:15.
[13] 1 Nephi 7:12, Moroni 10:23.

The Greatest Thing in the World

We are also told that God works in the lives of people that demonstrate faith in him.[14]

Moroni affirms that "it was by faith that Christ showed himself unto our fathers, after he had risen from the dead" and that Christ did not appear "unto them until after they had faith in him." [15]

The brother of Jared demonstrated sufficient faith to see the finger of his Lord and Savior. After he saw Christ's finger, the Lord asked him: "Sawest thou more than this?"

The brother of Jared replied: "Nay, Lord, show thyself unto me."

And when the Lord asked him: "Believest thou the words which I shall speak?" the brother of Jared firmly responded: "Yea, Lord, I know thou speakest the truth, for thou art a God of truth, and canst not lie." [16] Because of his faith, the veil was lifted, and the brother of Jared saw the spirit body of the Lord.

Additionally, one of our contemporary revelations to the Prophet Joseph Smith teaches us that without faith

---

[14] See Ether 12:30, 31.
[15] Ether 12:7.
[16] Ether 3:9-12.

"no man can please God."[17] The basis for this declaration is found in Mormon's words that "we are saved by faith in his name; and by faith [we] become the sons [and daughters] of God."[18] Consequently, Mormon powerfully and persuasively tells us: "If ye have not faith in him then ye are not fit to be numbered among the people of his church."[19]

Faith is a "principle of action in all intelligent beings."[20] As a principle of action, it is the force which makes things happen in our lives. Christ has stated: "If ye will have faith in me ye shall have power to do whatsoever thing is expedient in me."[21]

Greater than all of this, it was by faith that the "more excellent way," the atoning sacrifice of our Savior, was accomplished.[22]

That great word, faith, *has been the key-note for centuries of the popular religion; and we have easily learned to look upon it as the greatest thing in the world.*

Well, we are wrong.

In the 13th chapter of 1 Corinthians,

---

[17] D&C 63:11.
[18] Moroni 7:26.
[19] Moroni 7:39.
[20] Lectures on Faith 1:9.
[21] Moroni 7:33.
[22] Ether 12:11.

The Greatest Thing in the World

Paul takes us to

CHRISTIANITY AT ITS SOURCE;

and there we see, "The greatest of these is Charity."

The Book of Mormon prophet, Moroni, makes a concluding petition in his writings that we should come unto Christ and be perfected in him. This great prophet testified:

"Wheretofore, there must be faith; and if there must be faith there must also be hope; and if there must be hope there must also be charity. And except ye have charity ye can in nowise be saved in the kingdom of God; neither can ye be saved in the kingdom of God if ye have not faith; neither can ye if ye have no hope." [23]

Faith, hope, and charity are familiar expressions frequently used in conjunction with each other and almost always, it would appear, in that particular sequence, but perhaps we do not fully realize or understand why. When we demonstrate true faith in Jesus Christ and believe in His message, we, in due time, gain the incomparable

---

[23] Moroni 10:20, 21.

understanding that, through the Atonement, Christ can in reality save us from sin and death. We realize that there is hope for our lost and suffering souls.

When we believe in Christ, that is, when we have faith, it follows almost automatically that we would have hope in our own salvation and exaltation. The possibility and prospect of once again being with Christ and the Father brings an anticipation that we will also be like them. We cannot return to our Father without becoming like our Father and we know, as the scriptures testify, that God is love.

Having faith in Christ gives us hope of being with Him in the eternities and that hope drives our desire to be like Him. We begin to imitate and emulate His actions. We begin to treat others the way He treated others. We develop greater love for God and for others. We experience the gift of charity, the pure love of Christ.

The sequence becomes significant; if we have faith, it will give us hope and lead us to love. [24] Paul suggests that charity, being mentioned last, is also the greatest of the three. [25]

---

[24] See John 13:35.
[25] See 1 Corinthians 13:13.

The Greatest Thing in the World

It is not an oversight. Paul was speaking of faith just a moment before. He says, "If I have all faith, so that I can remove mountains, and have not Charity, *I am nothing." So far from forgetting, he deliberately contrasts them, "Now abideth Faith, Hope,* Charity,*" and without a moment's hesitation the decision falls, "The greatest of these is* Charity."

If Paul is correct in his writing, then charity is greater than faith. What a bold and powerful pronouncement considering all the miraculous accomplishments realized through the power of faith. Charity is the essence of the gospel of Jesus Christ. It is the conduct, demeanor and personification of the Savior. As Mormon stated: charity is the pure love of Christ. [26]

And it is not prejudice. A man is apt to recommend to others his own strong point. Charity or *Love was not Paul's strong point.*

Paul was a devout Jew from the city of Tarsus, one of the most influential cities in Asia Minor. Paul referred to himself as being "of the stock of Israel, of the tribe of

---

[26] Moroni 7:47.

Benjamin, a Hebrew of the Hebrews; as touching the law, a Pharisee." [27] Paul is well known for taking an active part in the martyrdom of Stephen. [28] He confesses that beyond measure he "violently persecuted" [29] the church of God.

The observing student can detect a beautiful tenderness growing and ripening all through his character as Paul gets old; but the hand that wrote, "The greatest of these is Charity," *when we meet it first, is stained with blood.*
Nor is this letter to the Corinthians peculiar in singling out Charity *as the summum bonum. The masterpieces of Christianity are agreed about it. Peter says, "Above all things have fervent love among yourselves." Above all things.*

Above all the attributes of godliness and perfection, charity is the one most fervently and earnestly to be sought after.

And John goes farther, "God is love."

Charity, the pure love of Christ, is

---

[27] Philippians 3:5.
[28] Acts 7:58-60, 22:20.
[29] Galatians 1:13, 14.

eternal love, perfect love, a love which lasts forever. It is love so fixed and focused in righteousness that it lifts our purpose, our aspirations, to the singular eternal welfare of our own soul and the souls of all those around us. [30] When we have charity, we are absorbed and engaged by it in all that we do. It becomes the dominant, fundamental purpose of our existence.

Thomas S. Monson stated that: "In a hundred small ways, all of [us] wear the mantle of charity. Life is perfect for none of us. Rather than being judgmental and critical of each other, may we have the pure love of Christ for our fellow travelers in this journey through life. May we recognize that each one is doing their best to deal with the challenges which come their way, and may we strive to do our best to help out." [31]

To be disciples of Christ, we must possess the supreme gift of charity.

You remember the profound remark which Paul makes elsewhere, "Love is the fulfilling of the law." Did you ever think what he meant by that?

---

[30] See 2 Nephi 26:30, Moroni 7:47, 8:25,26.
[31] Monson, Thomas S., General Conference, October 2010.

Frequently our involvement with charity is limited to merely reciting the words of Paul, Mormon or even Alma, without a conscientious consideration of their intended meaning. How many of us actively and purposefully seek the gift of charity? Some of us have been compared to "a door swinging on its hinges without any real interest in" the subject of this greatest gift of God. President George Q. Cannon observed that: "We find, even among those who have embraced the Gospel, hearts of unbelief." [32]

We should demonstrate a diligence, an active faith and a constant seeking for this gift of charity which is the fulfillment of the law. We all encounter myriad occasions daily to perform acts of kindness that will create an eternal difference in the lives of others as well as in our own. Anne Pingree suggests that "we can alter the face of the earth one family and one home at a time through charity, our small and simple acts of pure love." [33] All too frequently, however, our display of kindness is allocated solely to close friends, neighbors, and Church members. We should demonstrate kindness with anyone and everyone with whom we associate on any given day.

---

[32] Source Unknown
[33] Internet Quote.

The Greatest Thing in the World

Before Christ came men were working the passage to Heaven by keeping the Ten Commandments, and the hundred and ten other commandments which they had manufactured out of them. Christ came and said, "I will show you a more simple way. If you do one thing, you will do these hundred and ten things, without ever thinking about them. If you love, you will unconsciously fulfill the whole law."

When we see the gospel as a specific set of rules and commandments requiring our immediate and undeviating observance, we can quickly become overwhelmed. Does perfection mean mastering thousands of little laws and performing them with exactness? Is this what we consider to be "enduring to the end?"

God has given us laws to obey and He has given us principles to live by. There is a significant difference between laws and principles. In the movie, *The Christmas Oranges*, a young orphan named Rose breaks one of the rules of the orphanage. As the director of the orphanage doles out her punishment, he explains to Rose that rules are rules. Rose replies: "And the rules must not be broken."

Rules are rigid. They must not be broken. Living by the rules would require a rule for every possible human situation. We would need more rules than anyone could ever learn or live by. Rules, like the law of Moses, become obsolete once we begin to live a principle-centered life.

You can readily see for yourselves how that must be so. Take any of the commandments.

"Thou shalt have no other gods before Me." If a man love God, you will not require to tell him that. Love is the fulfilling of that law.

"Take not His name in vain." Would he ever dream of taking His name in vain if he loved him?

"Remember the Sabbath day to keep it holy." Would he not be too glad to have one day in seven to dedicate more exclusively to the object of his affection? Love would fulfill all these laws regarding God.

And so, if he loved man, you would never think of telling him to honor his father and mother. He could not do anything else.

It would be preposterous to tell him not to kill.

You could only insult him if you suggested that he should not steal—how could he steal from those he loved?

It would be superfluous to beg him not to bear false witness against his neighbor. If he loved him it would be the last thing he would do.

And you would never dream of urging him not to covet what his neighbors had. He would rather they possessed it than himself.

Charity includes within it all the other commandments. Paul wrote: "He that loveth another hath fulfilled the law. For this, Thou shalt not kill, Thou shalt not steal, Thou shalt not bear false witness, Thou shalt not covet; and if there be any other commandment, it is briefly comprehended in this saying, namely, Thou shalt love thy neighbour as thyself. Love worketh no ill to his neighbour: therefore love is the fulfilling of the law." [34]

Rules, laws and commandments do not require much wisdom or thought from those who keep them. They are pre-determined, perfunctory and mechanistic. The Ten Commandments were given to a spiritually immature Israel because they could not live the higher principles of the gospel.

Because of the adaptability and

---

[34] Romans 13:8-10.

flexibility of higher, principle-centered living, spiritual maturity and judgment are essential. When asked how he could govern so many Latter-day Saints, Joseph Smith responded: "I teach them correct principles and they govern themselves." Joseph taught the principles and the Latter-day Saint people employed those principles in their daily living.

Commandments, laws, and rules all have their place. Some find it easier, in the beginning, to follow a set of rules. These laws can be a training program that teaches us the particulars of God's ultimate expectations for us. Some find it easier to evaluate personal progress along the covenant path from the perspective of "obeying all the rules" while progressing toward always being obedient to all of God's laws. [35] The many and numerous laws of God are each good, important, and true in their own right, but Paul teaches us "a more excellent way." [36] One single principle encompasses all the rules, laws and commandments ever spoken. If we live this one "royal law" as James calls it, [37] we automatically live all the commandments. [38]

---

[35] See Galatians 3:24.
[36] 1 Corinthians 12:31.
[37] James 2:8.
[38] See 1 Peter 4:8; Romans 4:7, 8.

That principle is charity, the pure love of Christ.

In this way "Love is the fulfilling of the law." It is the rule for fulfilling all rules, the new commandment for keeping all the old commandments, Christ's one

SECRET OF THE CHRISTIAN LIFE.

The great secret of the Christian life is not faith but charity.

"And now abideth faith, hope, charity, these three; but the greatest of these is charity." [39] "Above all things, clothe yourselves with the bond of charity, as with a mantle, which is the bond of perfectness and peace." [40] "Above all things have fervent charity among yourselves, for charity shall cover the multitude of sins." [41]

Charity is the *summum bonum*, the crowning virtue, the supreme good, the prime directive, "the end of the commandment." [42]

Charity is a gift of the Spirit. We must have charity to have salvation. Moroni attests that "except ye have charity ye can in nowise

---

[39] 1 Corinthians 13:13.
[40] D&C 88:125, Colossians 3:14.
[41] 1 Peter 4:8.
[42] 1 Timothy 1:5.

be saved in the kingdom of God." [43]

Charity is an essential qualification for the ministers of Christ. [44] Jeffrey R. Holland pleads that "we give the God and Father of us all a helping hand with His staggering task of answering prayers, providing comfort, drying tears, and strengthening feeble knees. If we will do that," suggests Brother Holland, "we will be more like the true disciples of Christ we are meant to be." [45]

The gift of charity is the ultimate expression of Christ's love. It doesn't matter if that gift comes directly from Christ Himself or from those who serve him. There is no greater gift and to be lifted and supported through the gift of charity should motivate us to in turn lift and bless and support others. Neill F. Marriot advises that "Heavenly Father will help us love even those we may think are unloveable, if we plead for his aid. The Savior's Atonement is a conduit for the constant flow of charity from our father in heaven." [46]

Others can experience the gift of charity, the pure love of Christ, through us.

---

[43] Moroni 10:20,21.
[44] D&C 4:5.
[45] Holland, Jeffrey R., General Conference, April 2018.
[46] Source Unknown.

Think of it as the effect of a pebble tossed into a clear pond. Like the ripples on the water's surface, charity radiates outward in every direction. It disseminates from person to person and, having once reached the shore, it returns toward the source.

We are commanded to seek and attain charity. [47] We are asked to love one another the same way that Christ loves us. No one can rightfully perform the Lord's work without charity. [48]

The Savior told Moroni: "Faith, hope and charity bringeth unto me—the fountain of all righteousness." [49]

Moroni responded: "I remember that thou hast said that thou hast loved the world, even unto the laying down of thy life for the world, that thou mightest take it again to prepare a place for the children of men.

"And now I know that this love which thou hast had for the children of men is charity; wherefore, except men shall have charity they cannot inherit that place which thou hast prepared in the mansions of thy

---

[47] D&C 121:45, 124:116, 2 Nephi. 33:7-9, Alma 7:24, 1 Corinthians 16:14, 1 Timothy 4:12, 2 Timothy 2:22, Titus 2:2, 2 Peter 1:7.
[48] D&C 12:8, 18:19.
[49] Ether 12:28.

Father."[50]

Now Paul has learned that; and in this noble eulogy he has given us the most wonderful and original account extant of the summum bonum. We may divide it into three parts. In the beginning of the short chapter we have charity *contrasted; in the heart of it, we have* charity *analyzed; toward the end, we have* charity *defended as the supreme gift.*

---

[50] Ether 12:33, 34.

The Greatest Thing in the World

Chapter Two

THE CONTRAST

The concept of charity exists in every civilization and society. It epitomizes everything from a general love of others to the very specific giving of donations, gifts or offerings. The dictionary defines charity as "performing benevolent actions for the needy with no expectation of material reward." In other words, charity is seen as simply giving something to people who are in need. Churches, hospitals and other similar establishments are designated as "charitable" organizations because they are considered channels through which services to the needy are provided. Charitable acts, whether performed by individuals or organizations, are often associated with Christian service.

There is an enormous need for benevolent, philanthropic giving in the world today. It is a commodity in great demand. But "giving," suggests Kathy Calvin, "is not just about making a donation. It is about making a difference." [51] True charity differs greatly from what the world thinks of as charitable acts of giving.

The prophet Joseph Smith tells us that "It is a duty which every Saint ought to render to his brethren freely—to always love them and ever succor them." [52]

The restored doctrine revealed in the Book of Mormon defines charity as "the pure love of Christ, and it endureth forever; and whoso is found possessed of it at the last day, it shall be well with him." [53]

Marvin J. Ashton tells us that "real charity is not something you give away; it is something that you acquire and make a part of yourself. And when the virtue of charity becomes implanted in your heart, you are never the same again." [54]

---

[51] Source Unknown.
[52] Smith, Joseph, *History of the Church* 2:229.
[53] Moroni 7:47, Ether 12:34, 2 Nephi 26:30.
[54] Ashton, Marvin J., *The Tongue Can Be a Sharp Sword*, Ensign, May 1992.

The Greatest Thing in the World

The word 'charity' when used in context of the restored gospel never denotes the simple giving of money, goods or deeds of benevolence. It may be the motivating factor behind the giving, but we have come to understand that charity is so much more than simply sharing something with the less fortunate. It is, in fact, precisely what Henry Drummond's little book claims it to be, the greatest thing in the world.

Mormon designates charity as "the greatest of all." [55] It is the prime directive, the crowning virtue, the summum bonum of a divine character. Anyone seeking to become more like the Savior, to love as He loved, will seek the gift of charity. Its sole concern is the eternal welfare and the incessant happiness of others.

The Book of Mormon decrees: "Charity is the pure love of Christ." [56] As such, charity is exemplified as:

- selfless and self-sacrificing, [57]
- stemming from a pure heart, a good conscience, and faith unfeigned. [58]

---

[55] Moroni 7:46.

[56] Moroni 7:47.

[57] 1 Corinthians 13:5.

[58] 1 Timothy 1:5.

Charity has no selfish qualities. True charity implies a sincere love of others. Bruce C. Hafen, author of *The Broken Heart*, recognized that: "Our own internally generated compassion for the needs of others is a crucial indication of our desire to be followers of the Savior." [59] Charity causes our hearts to go out to others in pure, sincere love. It instills within us a desire to lift, sustain, build-up and support all those around us with the ultimate aim of directing them to a better life on Earth and an eventual existence in the celestial realm with God. Charity demands that we love others in the same way in which God loves them.

It is important to remember that we will never look into the eyes of someone whom God does not love. Bruce C. Hafen continues: "For that reason, we must be reaching out to others even as we reach out to God, rather than waiting to respond to others' needs until our charitable instincts are quickened by the Spirit. But even then, charity in its full-blown sense is 'bestowed upon' Christ's righteous followers. Its source, like all other blessings of the Atonement, is the grace of God." [60]

We cannot be capable, profitable

---

[59] Hafen, Bruce C., *The Broken Heart*, p. 195.
[60] Ibid., p. 196.

servants until we learn to demonstrate compassion, kindness and understanding to all of God's children. Many people yearn for this kind of love and recognize when it is extended to them.

Charity, the pure love of Christ, is more than an act or a deed we do. It is an attitude we carry within ourselves at all times. Charity is a state of the heart and of the mind [61] that carries over into everything we do and is offered to everyone we meet—unconditionally. [62]

Christ freed humanity from this world through pure love. Through his divine example he demonstrated we can achieve our highest potential only through kindness and charity toward others. Like Jesus, we can live the simple doctrine of kindness and of doing good to others, both to our friends as well as to our enemies.

As Thomas S. Monson suggests: "There is a serious need for the charity that gives attention to those who are unnoticed, hope to those who are discouraged, aid to those who are afflicted. True charity is love in action." [63]

We learn from Paul and from Moroni

---

[61] 1 Corinthians 13:4-7.
[62] D&C 121:45.
[63] My Inspirational Toolbox, Week 3.

that unless the love of God dwells in our hearts, we do not possess true charity. The depth and breadth of the gospel of Jesus Christ is to love and serve others. The foundation of all human relationships as seen from a gospel perspective is this "bond of perfectness and peace." [64] Charity is meant to be a part of our nature. We are instructed to:

- cleave unto it, [65]
- be clothed in it, [66]

The reason for this is that charity
- covers sins, [67]
- casts out fears, [68]
- is a prerequisite for entering the kingdom of Heaven. [69]

All things, in fact, are to be done in charity. Members of the Church of Jesus Christ of Latter-day Saints, more so than any other people on this planet, should cultivate charity. We profess to have the fullness of the gospel. When our behavior contradicts our claim, our hypocrisy and our ignorance

---

[64] Colossians 3:14, D&C 88:125.
[65] Moroni 7:46.
[66] D&C 88:125.
[67] 1 Peter 4:8.
[68] Moroni 8:17.
[69] Ether 12:34, Moroni 10:21.

become more apparent and pronounced.

Elaine Dalton indicates that "we often think of charity as an action. But I think of charity as a state of the heart." [70] Greatness is not measured by what we have, but by what we give.

Paul begins by contrasting Charity *with other things that men in those days thought much of. I shall not attempt to go over these things in detail. Their inferiority is already obvious.*

He contrasts it with eloquence. And what a noble gift it is, the power of playing upon the souls and wills of men, and rousing them to lofty purposes and holy deeds! Paul says, "If I speak with the tongues of men and of angels, and have not charity, *I am become sounding brass, or a tinkling cymbal." We all know why. We have all felt the brazenness of words without emotion, the hollowness, the unaccountable unpersuasiveness, of eloquence behind which lies no* Charity.

He contrasts it with prophecy. He contrasts it with mysteries. He contrasts it with faith. He contrasts it with alms. *Why is* Charity *greater than faith? Because the end is greater than the means. And why is it*

---

[70] Source unknown.

greater than offerings or hand-outs? *Because the whole is greater than the part.*

Charity *is greater than faith, because the end is greater than the means. What is the use of having faith? It is to connect the soul with God. And what is the object of connecting man with God? That he may become like God. But God is Love. Hence Faith, the means, is in order to Love, the end. Love* or Charity, *therefore, obviously is greater than faith. "If I have all faith, so as to remove mountains, but have not* Charity, *I am nothing."*

It is greater than benevolent offerings or philanthropy, *again, because the whole is greater than a part.* Altruism *is only a little bit of* Charity, *one of the innumerable avenues of* Charity, *and there may even be, and there is, a great deal of* altruism *without* Charity.

We can easily find people, everywhere throughout the world, who are willing to impart of their substance to the poor. But it is also often the case that these same people will show contempt for anyone who differs from them in matters of religion, politics or other subjects. Many people, noted for their hospitality, have shown intense hatred and bitterness toward others for reasons as simple as a difference of opinion.

Thomas S. Monson has instructed us that "charity is having patience with someone who has let us down. It is resisting the impulse to become offended easily. It is accepting weaknesses and shortcomings. It is accepting people as they truly are. It is looking beyond physical appearances to attributes that will not dim through time. It is resisting the impulse to categorize others." [71]

It is a very easy thing to toss a copper to a beggar on the street; it is generally an easier thing than not to do it. Yet Charity *is just as often in the withholding. We purchase relief from the sympathetic feelings roused by the spectacle of misery, at the copper's cost. It is too cheap—too cheap for us, and often too dear for the beggar. If we really loved him we would either do more for him, or less. Hence, "If I bestow all my goods to feed the poor, but have not* Charity *it profiteth me nothing."*

Service to others sanctifies us. In fact, it is essential to our salvation. Charity, however, is more than mere service. It is even more than self-sacrificing service. Charity is

---

[71] Source Unknown.

a manifestation of the Spirit of God. It is not just service, but it is the appropriate and proper incentive for our service to others.

Brother Hafen explains that: "The ultimate purpose of the gospel of Jesus Christ is to cause the sons and daughters of God to become as Christ is. Those who see religions purpose only in terms of ethical service in the relationship between man and fellowmen may miss that divinely ordained possibility. It is quite possible to render charitable—even 'Christian'—service without developing a deeply ingrained and permanent Christlike character. Paul understood this when he warned against giving all one's goods to feed the poor without true charity.

"We can give without loving, but we cannot love without giving. If our vertical relationship with God is complete, then, by the fruit of that relationship, the horizontal relationship with our fellow beings will also be complete. We then act charitably toward others, not merely because we think we should, but because that is the way we are.

"Service to others will surely bring us closer to God, especially when motivated by an unselfish sense of personal compassion. But even such desirable service will not of itself complete our relationship with God, because it will not by itself result in the bestowal of the complete attributes of godliness. That bestowal requires the ordinances and doctrines of the restored gospel and all the other elements of sacrifice and obedience spelled out in the scriptures. For that reason, while religions philosophies whose highest aim is social relevance may do much good, they will not ultimately lead people to achieve the highest religious purpose, which is to become as God and Christ are." [72]

While it is imperative that we develop the gift of charity so that we can bless the lives of others, the paramount and supreme purpose of charity is to make us more like our Lord and Savior.

Then Paul contrasts Charity *with sacrifice and martyrdom: "If I give my body to be burned, but have not* Charity, *it profiteth me nothing." Missionaries can take nothing greater to the* gentile *world than the impress and reflection of the Love of God upon their own character. That is the universal language. It will take them years to speak in Chinese, or in the dialects of India. From the day they land, that language of* Charity, *understood by all, will be pouring forth its*

---

[72] Hafen, Bruce C., *The Broken Heart*, pp. 196-197.

unconscious eloquence.

It is the man who is the missionary, it is not his words. His character is his message. In the heart of Africa, among the great Lakes, I have come across African *men and women who remembered the only* Caucasian *they ever saw before—David Livingstone; and as you cross his footsteps in that dark continent,*

MEN'S FACES LIGHT UP

as they speak of the kind doctor who passed there years ago. They could not understand him; but they felt the love that beat in his heart. They knew that it was love, although he spoke no word.

As a young boy I read the book, *Matthew Cowley: Man of Faith.* This book could have been just as appropriately titled, *Matthew Cowley: Man of Charity.* At age 17, Elder Cowley was called to serve as a missionary. His original assignment was to serve in Hawaii, but it was subsequently changed to New Zealand instead. There, he developed an extraordinary ability with the Māori language and a great love for the people. His mission lasted five years. After he returned home, he continued to write letters to the Māori people throughout his life.

In 1938, Elder Cowley was called to serve as president of the New Zealand Mission and was able to visit with many of the people he had met on his first mission. As World War II began, the Church called the missionaries serving overseas back home to the United States, but Elder Cowley and his family remained in New Zealand throughout the war. He was affectionately called "tumuaki," meaning president, by the Māori members and he performed many miracles while serving there. Elder Cowley was known by both members and non-members alike for his sincere love and dedication to the Māori people. Elder Cowley understood and lived the principle of charity.

Paul taught that charity is more than simply giving food to the hungry, clothes to the needy or comfort to the afflicted.

"Though I bestow all my goods to feed the poor, and though I give my body to be burned, and have not charity, it profiteth me nothing. Charity suffereth long, and is kind; charity envieth not; charity vaunteth not itself, is not puffed up; doth not behave itself unseemly, seeketh not her own, is not easily provoked, thinketh no evil; rejoiceth not in iniquity, but rejoiceth in the truth; beareth all things, believeth all things, hopeth all things, endureth all things. Charity never faileth." [73]

If charity consists of possessing all the above-mentioned characteristics, then this world is certainly suffering from a famine of charity today. Few of us exemplify all the traits attributed to charity in these verses from Paul.

Do we "suffer long" and without a complaint, even when the cause of our suffering is someone returning evil for good? Jeffery R. Holland reminds us that "when life is hard, remember—we are not the first to ask, 'Is there no other way?'" [74]

Are we kind to those who are cruel to us? If we genuinely love God, then the fruit of that love will be a love for our fellow beings. Kindness is extremely powerful. Russell M. Nelson taught that "there is power in our love for God and for His children, and when that love is tangibly manifest in millions of acts of Christian kindness, it will sweeten and nourish the world with the life-sustaining nectar of faith, hope and charity." [75]

"The nearer we get to our heavenly

---

[73] 1 Corinthians 13:3-8.
[74] Source Unknown.
[75] Nelson, Russell M., *Be Anxiously Engaged*, Ensign Nov. 2012.

Father," Joseph Smith stated, "the more we are disposed to look with compassion on perishing souls; we feel that we want to take them upon our shoulders, and cast their sins behind our backs…. If you would have God have mercy on you, have mercy on one another." [76]

Do we ever envy a neighbor's fancy clothes, fine home or new car, or the accolades and salaries enjoyed by others? Socrates called envy "the ulcer of the soul." [77]

Do any of us live with celebrity status, under a wave of prosperity and in the lap of luxury, and "vaunteth not" themselves, are "not puffed up" with pride or "doth not behave unseemly?" Charity will always conquer pride. Ezra Taft Benson taught us that "pride is a sin that is readily seen in others but is rarely admitted in ourselves." [78]

Do we "seeketh not" tour own, "but rather" prefer others before ourselves?

Are we "easily provoked?" Do we retaliate against those who offend us in some way or another?

Do we "think not evil" of those who

---

[76] Smith, Joseph, *History of the Church*, Vol. 5, pp. 23, 24.

[77] Source Unknown.

[78] Source Unknown.

go contrary to our views?

Latter-day Saints, as well or better than any people, understand deep-seated prejudice. Not many people have had extermination orders issued against them, making it legal to murder them for no reason whatsoever. And yet, how many, even among the Saints, fully and befittingly "bear all things" and prove themselves to be truly Christ-like?

How many of us would prefer to suffer wrong than to do wrong?

King Benjamin challenges us to become as little children: "submissive, meek, humble, patient, full of love, willing to submit to all things which the Lord seeth fit to inflict" upon us. [79] And Alma instructs us that we should humble ourselves "before the Lord, and call on his holy name, and watch and pray continually, that ye may not be tempted above that which ye can bear, and thus be led by the Holy Spirit, becoming humble, meek, submissive, patient, full of love and all long-suffering; having faith on the Lord; having a hope that ye shall receive eternal life; having the love of God always in your hearts, that ye may be lifted up at the last day and enter into his rest." [80]

---

[79] Mosiah 3:19.
[80] Alma 13:28.

The Greatest Thing in the World

Charity has been called the highest of all the spiritual gifts and the capstone of spiritual endowments. As we have said, Paul refers to it as "a more excellent way" [81] To be filled with charity is to be clothed in the mantle of perfectness and peace. [82]

Take into your sphere of labor, where you also mean to lay down your life, that simple charm of charity, *and your lifework must succeed. You can take nothing greater, you need take nothing less. You may take every accomplishment; you may be braced for every sacrifice; but if you give your body to be burned, and have not* Charity, *it will profit you and the cause of Christ nothing.*

Mormon's statement regarding charity included some language omitted by Paul: "If a man be meek and lowly in heart, and confesses by the power of the Holy Ghost that Jesus is the Christ, he must needs have charity; for if he have not charity he is nothing; wherefore he must needs have charity.

"And charity suffereth long, and is kind, and envieth not, and is not puffed up, seeketh not her own, is not easily provoked,

---

[81] 1 Corinthians 12:31.
[82] See D&C 88:125.

thinketh no evil, and rejoiceth not in iniquity but rejoiceth in the truth, beareth all things, believeth all things, hopeth all things, endureth all things.

"Wherefore, my beloved brethren, if ye have not charity, ye are nothing, for charity never faileth. Wherefore, cleave unto charity, which is the greatest of all, for all things must fail—

"But charity is the pure love of Christ, and it endureth forever; and whoso is found possessed of it at the last day, it shall be well with him.

"Wherefore, my beloved brethren, pray unto the Father with all the energy of heart, that ye may be filled with this love, which he hath bestowed upon all who are true followers of his Son, Jesus Christ; that ye may become the sons of God; that when he shall appear we shall be like him, for we shall see him as he is; that we may have this hope; that we may be purified even as he is pure." [83]

These verses are intended to emphasize the superlative status of charity among the attributes of godliness. Both Paul and Mormon write as though having faith to move mountains is nothing compared to charity. The emphasis is that there is nothing

---

[83] Moroni 7:44-48.

so excellent as possessing this pure love of Christ.

This is the heart of the matter: Charity is a gift of the Spirit. It motivates us to greater goodness, specifically greater service and compassion for others. We know that it is possible to serve people without loving them; but we also understand that we cannot truly love others without serving them. Service is essential to salvation. As Christians, we have a covenantal obligation to serve others. [84] But service is not the same as charity. Charity is the loftiest, noblest and deepest form of love. It is not mere affection; it is the pure love of Christ.

The love that Jesus Christ has for all of us is charity. [85] Charity is a pure love of others, similar to Christ's love for us. It is also loving Christ with a pure love. Pure love comes from a pure source; it comes from God.

"Charity is three-dimensional," writes John Bytheway. "It encompasses love for Christ, love from Christ, and love like Christ. In other words, to experience the pure love of Christ means to feel Christ's love for

---

[84] See Mosiah 18:8-10, James 2:8.
[85] See Ether 12:34.

you, to love Christ purely yourself, and to love others purely as Christ loves them." [86]

We cannot produce or engender such a love on our own. It is a gift of the Spirit. As a gift of the Spirit, charity is bestowed by God. Charity, the "more excellent way," [87] comes by and through the Holy Ghost.

Charity is symbolized by the tree of life seen in Lehi's vision; it is the love of God which "sheddeth itself abroad in the hearts of the children of men." [88] Those who become sons and daughters of Jesus Christ, who have applied the atoning blood of the Savior and have been born again, are the ones upon whom the Lord bestows this gift. The true intent and objective of charity is not just to motivate us to Christian service, but also to sanctify us from sin and prepare us to be with God and be like God.

The time will come when we will be given all knowledge and the gifts of prophecy and revelation will no longer serve their rightful functions. These gifts shall be swallowed up in something greater and shall no longer be needed. When we become as God and know all things—past, present, and future—there will be no need for the gift of

---

[86] Bytheway, John, LDS Living.
[87] See 1 Corinthians 12:31.
[88] 1 Nephi 11:22.

prophesy. When we can speak all languages, there will be no need for the gifts of tongues. But some gifts will last forever: Faith, the power of God himself; hope, the assurance of eternal life and everlasting progression; and charity, the pure love of Christ.

Neal A. Maxwell tells us that "no love is ever wasted. It's worth does not lie in reciprocity." [89]

The time will never come throughout all eternity when charity does not burn brightly in the hearts of the hallowed and the souls of the sanctified. The only way we can qualify to be with our Father in heaven is to be transformed by the blood of Christ through the Holy Ghost, so that we become sons and daughters of Christ. Then we will be like him and we will live with him.

Speaking of that wonderous day the Psalmist wrote: "As for me, I will behold thy face in righteousness: I shall be satisfied, when I awake, with thy likeness." [90]

---

[89] Source Unknown.
[90] Psalms 17:15.

The Greatest Thing in the World

The Greatest Thing in the World

Chapter Three

THE ANALYSIS

The restored gospel of Jesus Christ reveals that faith, hope and charity constitute the groundwork for our spiritual growth. Mormon makes it clear that unless we possess these three qualities, especially charity, we are nothing. [91] Faith, hope, and charity are essential characteristics to becoming Christ-like. [92]

After contrasting Charity *with other spiritual gifts, Paul, in three very short verses, gives us an amazing analysis of what*

---

[91] Moroni 7:44.
[92] Ether 12:28.

this supreme thing is.

I ask you to look at it. It is a compound thing, he tells us. It is like light. As you have seen a man of science take a beam of light and pass it through a crystal prism, as you have seen it come out on the other side of the prism broken up into its component colors—red, and blue, and yellow, and violet, and orange, and all the colors of the rainbow—so Paul passes this thing, Charity, *through the magnificent prism of his inspired intellect, and it comes out on the other side broken up into its elements.*

In these few words we have what one might call

THE SPECTRUM OF CHARITY,

the analysis of Charity. *Will you observe what its elements are? Will you notice that they have common names; that they are virtues which we hear about every day; that they are things which can be practiced by every man* and every woman *in every place in life; and how, by a multitude of small things and ordinary virtues, the supreme thing, the summum bonum, is made up?*

The Spectrum of Charity *has nine ingredients:*

The Greatest Thing in the World

1. *Patience*   *"Charity suffereth long."*
2. *Kindness*   *"And is kind."*
3. *Generosity*   *"Charity envieth not."*
4. *Humility*   *"Charity vaunteth not itself, is not puffed up."*
5. *Courtesy*   *"Doth not behave itself unseemly."*
6. *Unselfishness* *"Seeketh not its own."*
7. *Good temper* *"Is not provoked."*
8. *Guilelessness* *"Taketh not account of evil."*
9. *Sincerity*   *"Rejoiceth not in unrighteous-ness, but rejoiceth with the truth."*

Patience; kindness; generosity; humility; courtesy; unselfishness; good temper; guilelessness; sincerity—these make up the supreme gift, the stature of the perfect person.

Taking time to investigate and explore the definitions for the terms used in 1st Corinthians 13 and Moroni 7 will give us a richer and a purer understanding of the characteristics of charity. This can be a very instructive, edifying and enlightening experience for anyone willing to put in the effort. Henry Drummond painstakingly examined the qualities and characteristics of charity and thought carefully about each one.

The Greatest Thing in the World

You will observe that all are in relation to people, *in relation to life, in relation to the known to-day and the near to-morrow, and not to the unknown eternity.*

We hear much of love to God; Christ spoke much of love to man.

We make a great deal of peace with heaven; Christ made much of peace on earth.

Religion is not a strange or added thing, but the inspiration of the secular life, the breathing of an eternal spirit through this temporal world. The supreme thing, in short, is not a thing at all, but the giving of a further finish to the multitudinous words and acts which make up the sum of every common day.

Patience. *This is the normal attitude of Charity;* Charity *passive,* Charity *waiting to begin; not in a hurry; calm; ready to do its work when the summons comes, but meantime wearing the ornament of a meek and quiet spirit.* Charity *suffers long; beareth all things; believeth all things; hopeth all things. For* Charity *understands, and therefore waits.*

Elder Dieter F. Uchtdorf explains that "patience is a godly attribute that can heal souls, unlock treasures of knowledge and understanding, and transform ordinary men and women into saints and angels. Patience is truly a fruit of the Spirit." [93]

Paul, together with the prophet Mormon, depicts the charitable person as long-suffering, bearing all things; given, in a small measure perhaps, the patience and perspective of Deity toward people, circumstances and surroundings; endowed with an eternal perspective where the present is greatly influenced by the knowledge of things to come. "Patience and perseverance are part of our eternal progression," stated Russel M. Nelson. [94]

Long suffering means to endure, bear, allow, permit, tolerate. Job suffered long, as did our Savior, Jesus Christ. Joseph Smith, the great prophet of the restoration, suffered long. Countless others have also been long-suffering. It was this quality of long suffering, enthused by the pure love of Christ, that allowed the sons of Mosiah to endure the persecution and rejection they faced among the Lamanites. [95] As Joyce Meyer explains: "Patience is not the ability to wait but to keep

---

[93] Uchtdorf, Dieter F., *Continue in Patience*, Ensign, May 2010.
[94] Nelson, Russel M., Ask, Seek, Knock. Ensign, October 2009.
[95] See Mosiah 28:3.

a good attitude while waiting." [96]

"Patience is a process of perfection," Dieter F. Uchtdorf stated. "The lessons we learn from patience will cultivate our character, lift our lives, and heighten our happiness." [97]

The Doctrine and Covenants advises us to "continue in patience." [98] The reason for this is, as Neal A. Maxwell explains: "Patience is tied very closely with faith in our Heavenly Father. Actually, when we are unduly impatient, we are suggesting that we know what is best—better than does God. Or, at least, we are asserting that our timetable is better than His. We can grow in faith only if we are willing to wait patiently for God's purposes and patterns to unfold in our lives, on His timetable." [99]

Joseph B. Wirthlin suggests that: "We will have genuine joy and happiness only as we learn patience." [100]

Kindness. Charity *active. Have you ever noticed how much of Christ's life was spent*

---

[96] Internet Quote.
[97] Uchtdorf, Dieter F., *Continue in Patience*, Ensign, May 2010.
[98] D&C 67:13.
[99] Maxwell, Neal A., *Patience*, Ensign, October 1980.
[100] Internet Quote.

in doing kind things—in merely doing kind things? Run over it with that in view, and you will find that He spent a great proportion of His time simply in making people happy, in

DOING GOOD TURNS

to people. There is only one thing greater than happiness in the world, and that is holiness; and it is not in our keeping; but what God has put in our power is the happiness of those about us, and that is largely to be secured by our being kind to them.

"Kindness is the essence of a celestial life," explains Joseph B. Wirthlin. "Kindness is how a Christ-like person treats others. Kindness should permeate all of our words and actions at work, at school, at church, and especially in our homes. Jesus, our Savior, was the epitome of kindness and compassion." [101]

The prophet Joseph Smith advised that: "As you increase in innocence and virtue, as you increase in goodness, let your hearts expand, let them be enlarged towards others; you must be long-suffering, and bear

---

[101] Mormonchannel.org.

with the faults and errors of mankind." [102]

Charity is friendly, gentle, calm, softhearted, and generous. Charity induces people to be decent human beings, to be compassionate and to be cognizant and sensitive to the needs and desires of others.

People are the business of charity. When Ebenezer Scrooge flatters the ghost of his departed business partner, Jacob Marley, by telling him, "You were always a good man of business," Jacob desolately replies: "Business! Mankind was my business. The common welfare was my business; charity, mercy, forbearance, and benevolence, were, all, my business. The dealings of my trade were but a drop of water in the comprehensive ocean of my business!" [103]

People are the object of Christ-like love. The pure love Jesus held in His heart was inextricably linked to service, sacrifice and kindness to others. We cannot develop charity, the pure love of Christ, without following the same process followed and prescribed by the Savior.

"Every day of our lives," advises Thomas S. Monson, "...we are given opportunities to show love and kindness to

---

[102] Source Unknown.
[103] Dickens, Charles, *A Christmas Carol*, Fall River Press, p. 23.

those around us.... As we arise each morning let us determine to respond with more love and kindness to whatever might come our way." [104]

"One who is kind is sympathetic and gentle with others," stated President Ezra Taft Benson. "He is considerate of others' feelings and courteous in his behavior. He has a helpful nature. Kindness pardons others' weaknesses and faults [and] is extended to all—to the aged and the young, to animals, to those low of station as well as the high." [105]

"Everyone," explains Neil L. Anderson, "independent of his or her beliefs, deserves our kindness and consideration." [106]

Charity, the pure love of Christ, motivated Ammon, a prince in the house of Mosiah, to denounce the throne and to devotedly and benevolently serve King Lamoni and his family, gaining their trust, and being an instrument in their conversion to the gospel of Jesus Christ. [107]

"The greatest thing," says some one,

---

[104] Internet Quote.
[105] Benson, Ezra Taft, General Conference, October 1986.
[106] www.todaysthebestday.com.
[107] See Alma 17-19.

"a man can do for his Heavenly Father is to be kind to some of His other children."

Joseph Smith taught: "'A soft answer turneth away wrath,' says the wise man; and it will be greatly to the credit of the Latter-day Saints to show the love of God, by now kindly treating those who may have, in an unconscious moment, done wrong; for truly said Jesus, Pray for thine enemies." [108]

I wonder why it is that we are not all kinder than we are? How much the world needs it! How easily it is done! How instantaneously it acts! How infallibly it is remembered! How superabundantly it pays itself back—for there is no debtor in the world so honorable, so superbly honorable, as Charity. "Charity *never faileth."* Charity *is success,* Charity *is happiness,* Charity *is life.* "Love," *I say with Browning,* "is energy of life."

"For life, with all it yields of joy or woe
And hope and fear,
Is just our chance o' the prize of learning love,—
How love might be, hath been indeed, and

---

[108] Smith, Joseph. *Teachings of the Prophet.*

is."

Where Love is, God is. He that dwelleth in Love dwelleth in God. God is Love. Therefore love. Without distinction, without calculation, without procrastination, love. Lavish it upon the poor, where it is very easy; especially upon the rich, who often need it most; most of all upon our equals, where it is very difficult, and for whom perhaps we each do least of all. There is a difference between trying to please and giving pleasure. Give pleasure. Lose no chance of giving pleasure; for that is the ceaseless and anonymous triumph of a truly loving spirit. "I shall pass through this world but once. Any good thing, therefore, that I can do, or any kindness that I can show to any human being, let me do it now. Let me not defer it or neglect it, for I shall not pass this way again."

"Wise men," taught the prophet Joseph Smith, "ought to have understanding enough to conquer men with kindness." [109]

And Joseph B. Wirthlin explains that "kindness is the essence of greatness." [110] "Sometimes the greatest love," he also tells

---

[109] Smith, Joseph, *Teachings of the Prophet*, p. 21.
[110] lds.net.

us, "is not found in the dramatic scenes that poets and writers immortalize. Often, the greatest manifestations of love are simple acts of kindness and caring we extend to those we meet along the path of life." [111]

Generosity. *"Charity envieth not." This is love in competition with others. Whenever you attempt a good work you will find other men doing the same kind of work, and probably doing it better. Envy them not. Envy is a feeling of ill-will to those who are in the same line as ourselves, a spirit of covetousness and detraction. How little Christian work even is a protection against un-Christian feeling! That most despicable of all the unworthy moods which cloud a Christian's soul assuredly waits for us on the threshold of every work, unless we are fortified with this grace of magnanimity. Only one thing truly need the Christian envy—the large, rich, generous soul which "envieth not."*

Camilla Kimball advises us to "never suppress a generous thought." [112]

When we are filled with charity, we rejoice in what we *can* do, no matter how

---

[111] Wirthlin, Joseph B., LDS Living.
[112] Internet Quote.

great or how little. We also rejoice in what others can do. "There is joy," explained Henry B. Iryng, "in giving and receiving the generosity that God inspires." [113] Comparing and competing is too strenuous and exhausting. When we are incessantly placing ourselves above those around us, it creates an overwhelming emotional drain on our spiritual batteries.

Charity doesn't boast or brag or try to place itself above another. "The charity that hastens to proclaim its good deeds," states William Hutton, "ceases to be charity, and is only pride and ostentation." [114]

When we are filled with charity, we feel no discontent or ill will when we see someone better off than we are, and we have no desire to possess something that rightfully belongs to another person. When we are filled with Christ's love we are less concerned over worldly acquisitions or accolades. This is not because there is anything inherently evil in possessions, rewards or recognition but because our joy is already full in Christ. [115]

When the residents of the great and

---

[113] mormonchannel.org.
[114] Internet Quote.
[115] See D&C 101:36.

The Greatest Thing in the World

spacious building [116] chant and revile against us, it is charity, the pure love of Christ, that serves as an anchor to our souls, enabling us to disregard and overlook the taunting and the temptations of the world. Our happiness is found in simple pleasures and we relish in God's kindness and mercy toward us.

"Above all", counselled Russell M. Nelson, "do not be selfish! Generate a spirit of selflessness and generosity." [117]

And then, after having learned all that, you have to learn this further thing, **Humility**—*to put a seal upon your lips and forget what you have done. After you have been kind, after* Charity *has stolen forth into the world and done its beautiful work, go back into the shade again and say nothing about it.* Charity *hides even from itself.* Charity *waives even self-satisfaction.* "Charity *vaunteth not itself, is not puffed up." Humility*—Charity *hiding.*

Richard G. Scott referred to humility as "the precious soil of righteous character." [118]

What is Christ teaching us about

---

[116] See 1 Nephi 8.
[117] ChurchofJesusChrist.org.
[118] Scott, Richard G., LDS Living.

charity when He says: "He that is greatest among you shall be your servant?" [119] When He reminds us that being in the service of others is actually being in the service of God, [120] He is, in effect, instructing us on how to develop greater charity. Consider the charitable aspects of some of His other teachings:

Christ tells us that we should respect, value and appreciate others as we would our own selves. [121] "Being humble," explains Gordon B. Hinckley, "means recognizing that we are not on earth to see how important we can become, but to see how much difference we can make in the lives of others." [122]

Christ instructs us to remember the poor and needy in all things. [123] What do you imagine He means by "in all things?"

He commands that we share with those who have less than ourselves. [124] "The more capable we are," encourages Jeffery R. Holland, "the more humble we should be." [125]

---

[119] Matthew 23:11.
[120] See Mosiah 2:17-22.
[121] See D&C 38:24-27.
[122] Pinterest Quote.
[123] See D&C 52:40.
[124] See Mosiah 18:26-28.
[125] Internet Quote.

Christ asks that those of us who are strong help and support those who are weak. [126] And He gives us His promise that if we will humble ourselves before him, he will make weak things become strong. [127]

He wants us to feed His sheep—to treat others the same way that He, the Good Shepard, would treat them. [128]

When we are filled with charity, we acknowledge the hand of God in all things. [129]

We turn attention away from ourselves and toward God. We try to not take personal credit for good deeds and accomplishments. "We don't discover humility," explains Dieter F. Uchtdorf, "by thinking less *of* ourselves. We discover humility by thinking less *about* ourselves." [130]

We forsake pride. The Book of Mormon illustrates how pride became such a great stumbling block for the Nephites and how "the church began to fail in its progress." [131]

The Book of Mormon also

---

[126] See Romans 15:1.

[127] See Ether 12:27.

[128] John 21:16.

[129] See D&C 59:21.

[130] Uchtdorf, Dieter F., *Pride and the Priesthood*, Ensign, October 2010.

[131] Alma 4:10.

demonstrates that during this same period of pride and wickedness people were "succoring those who stood in need of their succor, such as imparting their substance to the poor and the needy, feeding the hungry, and suffering all manner of afflictions, for Christ's sake." [132]

Remember that pride is concerned with who is right and humility is concerned with what is right. [133]

And finally, the great benefit of humility is, as Steven E. Snow explains, that it "enables us to have broken hearts when we sin or make mistakes and makes it possible for us to repent." [134]

The fifth ingredient is a somewhat strange one to find in this summum bonum: **Courtesy***. This is* Charity *in society,* Charity *in relation to etiquette.* "Charity *does not behave itself unseemly."*

The possession of charity disallows statements, inferences or actions which are offensive, rude or inappropriate. As Jim Butcher said: "If you can't manage courtesy,

---

[132] Alma 4:13.

[133] Benson, Ezra Taft.

[134] ChurchofJesusChrist.org.

try silence." [135]

Politeness has been defined as love in trifles. Courtesy is said to be love in little things. And the one secret of politeness is to love.

Charity makes us more sympathetic toward each other. We are willing to forgive more freely and completely. We are often much too hard on ourselves and others. When we spend our precious moments on this planet rivaling and reproving, criticizing and condemning, denouncing and demeaning everything and everyone around us, we overlook the golden opportunities for friendships and forgiveness, service and assistance, harmony and humanity that would create such an abundance of blessings in our lives. Charity is how we lighten our own burdens while we also lighten the burdens of others.

"Life is short," stated Ralph Waldo Emerson, "but there is always time for courtesy." [136]

Charity *cannot behave itself unseemly. You can put the most untutored*

---

[135] Internet Quote.
[136] Pinterest Quote.

persons into the highest society, and if they have a reservoir of Charity *in their heart they will not behave themselves unseemly. They simply cannot do it. Carlisle said of Robert Burns that there was no truer gentleman in Europe than the ploughman-poet. It was because he loved everything—the mouse, and the daisy, and all the things, great and small, that God had made. So with this simple passport he could mingle with any society, and enter courts and palaces from his little cottage on the banks of the Ayr.*

"Respect is more than giving consideration of one's feelings," wrote Tom Baker. "It is showing common courtesy for another human being." [137] And Theodore Roosevelt added that "courtesy is as much a mark of a gentleman as courage." [138]

You know the meaning of the word "gentleman." It means a gentle man—a man who does things gently, with Charity. *That is the whole art and mystery of it. The gentle man cannot in the nature of things do an ungentle, an ungentlemanly thing. The ungentle soul, the inconsiderate, unsympathetic nature, cannot do anything*

---

[137] Picturequotes.com.
[138] BrainyQuote.

else. "Charity *doth not behave itself unseemly."*

One person referred to charity as "persuasive poise under provocation." Charity makes us meek. When our hearts are transformed through the gift of charity, we do not desire to express anger because we do not experience anger.

"A soft answer turneth away wrath; but grievous words stir up anger." [139] It is said that courtesy costs nothing but buys everything. "Nothing is ever lost by courtesy," wrote Erastus Wiman. "It is the cheapest of pleasures, costs nothing and conveys much." [140]

Unselfishness. *"*Charity *seeketh not her own." Observe: Seeketh not even that which is her own. In Britain the Englishman is devoted, and rightly, to his rights. But there come times when a man may exercise even*

THE HIGHER RIGHT

of giving up his rights.
Yet Paul does not summon us to give up our rights. Charity *strikes much deeper. It*

---

[139] Proverbs 15:1.
[140] Quotefancy.

would have us not seek them at all, ignore them, eliminate the personal element altogether from our calculations.

It is not hard to give up our rights. They are often eternal. The difficult thing is to give up ourselves. The more difficult thing still is not to seek things for ourselves at all. After we have sought them, bought them, won them, deserved them, we have taken the cream off them for ourselves already. Little cross then to give them up. But not to seek them, to look every man not on his own things, but on the things of others—that is the difficulty. "Seekest thou great things for thyself? said the prophet; "seek them not." Why? Because there is no "greatness in things." Things cannot be great. The only greatness is unselfish love. Even self-denial in itself is nothing, is almost a mistake. Only a great purpose or a mightier love can justify the waste.

"Our Savior gave Himself in unselfish service," declared Dallin H. Oaks. "He taught that each of us should follow Him by denying ourselves of selfish interests in order to serve others." [141]

---

[141] Oaks, Dallin H., General Conference, April 2009.

The Greatest Thing in the World

It is more difficult, I have said, not to seek our own at all than, having sought it, to give it up. I must take that back. It is only true of a partly selfish heart. Nothing is a hardship to Charity, *and nothing is hard. I believe that Christ's "yoke" is easy. Christ's yoke is just His way of taking life. And I believe it is an easier way than any other. I believe it is a happier way than any other. The most obvious lesson in Christ's teaching is that there is no happiness in having and getting anything, but only in giving. I repeat, there is no happiness in having or in getting, but only in giving. Half the world is on the wrong scent in pursuit of happiness. They think it consists in having and getting, and in being served by others. It consists in giving, and in serving others. "He that would be great among you," said Christ, "let him serve." He that would be happy, let him remember that there is but one way—"it is more blessed, it is more happy, to give than to receive."*

Charity reaches out to everyone everywhere under any given situation. Jesus never gave with the hope of getting something back. President Spencer W. Kimball stated: "Never did the Savior give in expectation." [142] True charity, the kind of charity that Jesus Himself taught and lived by, requires giving of ourselves. We can give food, money, or material goods that will often satisfy a critical need for another, but often an even more critical need is our mandate for self-sacrifice without the expectation of a return on investment.

Jesus was at all times a giver yet rarely a recipient. Never did He require a trade or a deal. There was no negotiation, no "I'll do this for you if you'll do that for me." The nature of His gifts could never be repaid by the receiver. They were too precious and too priceless.

He didn't give bath soaps; He gave cleanliness to the unclean.

He didn't give scented candles; He gave light in the darkness.

He didn't give designer shoes; He gave legs to the lame.

He didn't give concert tickets; He gave ears to the deaf.

He didn't give an eye-catching painting; He gave sight to the blind.

He didn't give a bowl of chicken-noodle soup; He gave healing to the sick.

He didn't give a visit to a prisoner; He

---

[142] Source Unknown.

gave freedom to the oppressed.

He didn't give a sweet-smelling perfume; He gave breath to the lifeless.

He didn't give mere acts of kindness; He gave forgiveness to the repentant.

His friends gave him food, shelter and companionship; He gave them His love, His service and His life.

Wise men gave Him gold, frankincense and myrrh; He gave them resurrection, salvation and eternal life.

None of us can give what Jesus gave but we can give *like* Jesus gave.

We can be the first to say hello or become acquainted with a stranger.

We can visit our neighbors, our friends and even people we don't know.

We can share our time with senior citizens who may feel forgotten or neglected.

We can learn to be listeners instead of talkers.

We can learn from children to be more child-like.

David O. McKay tells us that "true Christianity is love in action. There is no better way to manifest love for God than to show an unselfish love for one's fellow men." [143] In a heart that is filled with charity

---

[143] Relatably.com.

we will never find cliques or exclusive groups. All of us belong. All of us are welcome. All of us still have so much to learn about the selflessness of the pure love of Christ.

Franklin D. Roosevelt referred to selfishness as "the only true atheism" and "unselfishness, the only true religion." [144]

"A life filled with unselfish service," wrote Howard W. Hunter, "will also be filled with peace that surpasses understanding." [145]

The next ingredient is a very remarkable one: **Good temper.** *"Charity is not provoked."*

Nothing could be more striking than to find this here. We are inclined to look upon bad temper as a very harmless weakness. We speak of it as a mere infirmity of nature, a family failing, a matter of temperament, not a thing to take into very serious account in estimating a man's character. And yet here, right in the heart of this analysis of Charity, *it finds a place; and the Bible again and again returns to condemn it as one of the most destructive elements in human nature.*

---

[144] Source Unknown.
[145] Hunter, Howard W., Ensign, December 2002.

The development of charity inhibits the growth of anger, irritation, and impatience. When we have developed charity, we have developed a love for the Savior and a desire to love others as He does. Charity is more than a dictum, more than a mere word describing an abstract attribute or attitude. It is a tangible internal characteristic to be developed, experienced, and expressed in our outward actions toward others. Charity should be a part of our nature.

Gordon B. Hinckley pled with us to "control your tempers, put a smile upon your faces, which will erase anger; speak out with words of love and peace, appreciation, and respect. If you will do this, your lives will be without regret. Your marriages and family relationships will be preserved. You will be much happier. You will do greater good. You will feel a sense of peace that will be wonderful." [146]

Remember that anger is only one letter away from becoming danger.

The nature of charity can have a transforming effect on those around us. Joseph Smith declared that "Nothing is so much calculated to lead people to forsake sin as to take them by the hand, and watch over

---

[146] Hinckley, Gordon B., General Conference, October 2007.

them with tenderness. When persons manifest the least kindness and love to me, O what power it has over my mind, while the opposite course has a tendency to harrow up all the harsh feelings and depress the human mind." [147] Shame and humiliation, embarrassment, jealousy and resentment, revenge and retaliation, undeserved praise and unearned titles are all foreign to charity.

The peculiarity of ill temper is that it is the vice of the virtuous. It is often the one blot on an otherwise noble character. You know men who are all but perfect, and women who would be entirely perfect, but for an easily ruffled, quick-tempered, or "touchy" disposition. This compatibility of ill temper with high moral character is one of the strangest and saddest problems of ethics. The truth is, there are two great classes of sins—sins of the Body and sins of the Disposition.

The Prodigal Son may be taken as a type of the first, the Elder Brother of the second. Now, society has no doubt whatever as to which of these is the worse. Its brand falls, without a challenge, upon the Prodigal. But are we right? We have no balance to weigh one another's sins, and coarser and

---

[147] Smith Joseph, *Teachings of the Prophet*, p. 15.

finer are but human words; but faults in the higher nature may be less venal than those in the lower, and to the eye of Him who is Love, a sin against Charity *may seem a hundred times more base. No form of vice, not worldliness, not greed of gold, not drunkenness itself, does more to un-Christianize society than evil temper. For embittering life, for breaking up communities, for destroying the most sacred relationships, for devastating homes, for withering up men and women, for taking the bloom of childhood, in short,*

FOR SHEER GRATUITOUS MISERY-PRODUCING POWER

this influence stands alone.

Look at the Elder Brother—moral, hard-working, patient, dutiful—let him get all credit for his virtues—look at this man, this baby, sulking outside his own father's door. "He was angry," we read, "and would not go in." Look at the effect upon the father, upon the servants, upon the happiness of the guests. Judge of the effect upon the Prodigal—and how many prodigals are kept out of the Kingdom of God by the unlovely character of those who profess to be inside.

Analyze, as a study in Temper, the

thunder-cloud itself as it gathers upon the Elder Brother's brow. What is it made of? Jealousy, anger, pride, uncharity, cruelty, self-righteousness, touchiness, doggedness, sullenness—these are the ingredients of this dark and loveless soul. In varying proportions, also, these are the ingredients of all ill temper. Judge if such sins of the disposition are not worse to live in, and for others to live with, than the sins of the body. Did Christ indeed not answer the question Himself when He said, "I say unto you that the publicans and the harlots go into the Kingdom of Heaven before you?" There is really no place in heaven for a disposition like this. A man with such a mood could only make heaven miserable for all the people in it. Except, therefore, such a man be

BORN AGAIN,

he cannot, simply cannot, enter the kingdom of heaven.

You will see then why Temper is significant. It is not in what it is alone, but in what it reveals. This is why I speak of it with such unusual plainness. It is a test for Charity, *a symptom, a revelation of an unloving nature at bottom. It is the intermittent fever which bespeaks unintermittent disease within; the occasional bubble escaping to the surface which betrays some rottenness underneath; a sample of the most hidden products of the soul dropped involuntarily when off one's guard; in a word, the lightning form of a hundred hideous and un-Christian sins. A want of patience, a want of kindness, a want of generosity, a want of courtesy, a want of unselfishness, are all instantaneously symbolized in one flash of Temper.*

As we develop charity we become less "touchy" and less prone to display a quick temper. We are calm—not rushed and hurried in our approach with others. Charity takes time.

Charitable people look for the good in others. They forgive one another. The greatest example of forgiveness is demonstrated by our Savior. On the cross Christ forgave the soldiers that drove the nails into His hands and feet. "Father, forgive them," He implored, "For they know not what they do." [148] That was an act of pure love. We do not always know what we're doing either and all of us make mistakes. Maybe we should be a little more forgiving.

---

[148] Luke 23:34.

We could certainly all be a little more charitable.

Dietrich Bonhoeffer offered this council about bearing one another's burdens: "'Bear ye one another's burdens, and so fulfil the law of Christ,' [Paul commands us]. [149] The law of Christ, which it is our duty to fulfil, is the bearing of the cross. My brother's burden which I must bear is not only his outward lot… but quite literally his sin. And the only way to bear that sin is by forgiving it." [150]

The invitation to follow Christ is a sacred summon to forgive others. Bonhoeffer continues: "Forgiveness is the Christ-like suffering which it is the Christian's duty to bear." [151]

Elder Jeffrey R. Holland asks: "Is there someone in your life who perhaps needs forgiveness? Is there someone in your home, someone in your family, someone in your neighborhood who has done an unjust or an unkind or an unchristian thing? All of us are guilty of such transgressions, so there surely must be someone who yet needs your forgiveness.

---

[149] Galatians 6:2.
[150] Bonhoeffer, Dietrich, *The Cost of Discipleship*, p. 100.
[151] Ibid.

"And please don't ask if that's fair—that the injured should have to bear the burden of forgiveness for the offender. Don't ask if 'justice' doesn't demand that it be the other way around... You and I know that what we plead for is mercy—and that is what we must be willing to give." [152]

Elder Holland continues: "Surely the reason Christ said 'Father, forgive them' was because even in the weakened and terribly trying hour he faced, he knew that this was the message he had come through all eternity to deliver. All of the meaning and all of the majesty of all those dispensations—indeed the entire plan of salvation—would have been lost had he forgotten that not in spite of injustice and brutality and unkindness and disobedience but precisely because of them had he come to extend forgiveness to the family of man. Anyone can be pleasant and patient and forgiving on a good day. A Christian has to be pleasant and patient and forgiving on all days." [153]

Hence it is not enough to deal with the Temper. We must go to the source, and change the inmost nature, and the angry

---

[152] Holland, Jeffrey R., *I Stand All Amazed*, Ensign, August 1986, p. 72
[153] Ibid.

humors will die away of themselves. Souls are made sweet not by taking the acid fluids out, but by putting something in—a great Love, a new Spirit, the Spirit of Christ.

Christ, the Spirit of Christ, interpenetrating ours, sweetens, purifies, transforms all. This only can eradicate what is wrong, work a chemical change, renovate and regenerate, and rehabilitate the inner man. Will-power does not change men. Time does not change men.

CHRIST DOES.

Therefore, "Let that mind be in you which was also in Christ Jesus."

Some of us have not much time to lose. Remember, once more, that this is a matter of life or death. I cannot help speaking urgently, for myself, for yourselves. "Whoso shall offend one of these little ones, which believe in me, it were better for him that a millstone were hanged about his neck, and that he were drowned in the depth of the sea." That is to say, it is the deliberate verdict of the Lord Jesus that it is better not to live than not to love. It is better not to live than not to love.

Dieter F. Uchtdorf explains that

"whatever problems your family is facing, whatever you must do to solve them, the beginning and the end of the solution is charity, the pure love of Christ." [154]

***Guilelessness** and **Sincerity** may be dismissed almost without a word. Guilelessness is the grace for suspicious people. The possession of it is*

THE GREAT SECRET OF PERSONAL INFLUENCE.

You will find, if you think for a moment, that the people who influence you are people who believe in you. In an atmosphere of suspicion men shrivel up; but in that atmosphere they expand, and find encouragement and educative fellowship.

"Stay guileless," advises Nishi Tiwari. "You will have to remember less… and have access to inner peace." [155]

It is a wonderful thing that here and there in this hard, uncharitable world there should still be left a few rare souls who think

---

[154] Uchtdorf, Dieter F., General Conference, April 2016.
[155] Tiwari, Nishi, *Quotes and Writings by Nishi Tiwari*.

no evil. This is the great unworldliness. Charity *"thinketh no evil," imputes no motive, sees the bright side, puts the best construction on every action.*

"There is a strange glow on the face of a guileless person," writes spiritual Indian leader Sai Baba. "Inner cleanliness has its own soap and water—the soap of strong faith and the water of constant practice." [156]

What a delightful state of mind to live in! What a stimulus and benediction even to meet with it for a day! To be trusted is to be saved. And if we try to influence or elevate others, we shall soon see that success is in proportion to their belief of our belief in them. The respect of another is the first restoration of the self-respect a man has lost; our ideal of what he is becomes to him the hope and pattern of what he may become.

A loving and charitable person, while sickened by sin, desires to lift the sinner to holier ground.

In the fall of 1956, my father was called to serve as the Branch President of the Columbus, Ohio Branch of the Church of

---

[156] HoopoeQuotes.

Jesus Christ of Latter-day Saints. As my father began to consider who his counselors should be, he wrote in his journal: "I knew the Lord knew who He wanted in that position, and it was for me to find out…. As I knelt down to pray, the name of Harold Capener, who at the time was inactive in the Church, came very forcibly to my mind, with the feeling that he should be the counselor." My father went immediately, along with the District President, to Brother Capener's house to issue the call.

"Brother Capener, the Lord is calling you to be a counselor in the Columbus Branch Presidency. Will you accept the call?" asked the District President.

Brother Capener reacted as if he'd been hit in the stomach! "I can't do that," he replied. "I don't pay my tithing. I don't come to church. I don't keep the word of wisdom. I don't keep the Sabbath."

The District President told Brother Capener: "We are calling you to comply with all of those conditions."

After consulting with his wife, Brother Capener accepted the call and performed admirably. He later served as a member of the High Council, then, after moving to Ithaca, New York, was called to serve as District President. When a Stake was organized at Ithaca, Harold Capener was called as the first Stake President.

As strange as it sounds, it was Brother Capener's belief in my father's belief in Brother Capener that turned this man's life around. Or, more precisely, it was the Lord's belief in Brother Capener's abilities that inspired my father to look beyond his present lifestyle, to challenge him and to give him the hope to be more.

We are saddened, even distressed, by the world's waywardness and are always willing to assist any who wander from the paths of peace and righteousness.

Charity does not place us above or beneath others. We may abhor sin, [157] but we are filled with love for the sinner. In simple terms, don't treat people as bad as they are, treat them as good as you are.

"Charity rejoiceth not in unrighteousness, but rejoiceth with the truth." I have called this Sincerity from the words rendered in the Authorized Version by "rejoiceth in the truth." And, certainly, were this the real translation, nothing could be more just; for he who loves will love Truth not less than men. He will rejoice in the

---

[157] Alma 13:12.

Truth—rejoice not in what he has been taught to believe; not in this church's doctrine or in that; not in this -ism or in that -ism; but "in the Truth." He will accept only what is real; he will strive to get at facts; he will search for Truth with a humble and unbiased mind, and cherish whatever he finds at any sacrifice.

Charity rejoiceth in the truth, it rejoices in established facts. Brigham Young declared that the restored gospel "embraces all truth that is revealed and that is unrevealed, whether religious, political, scientific, or philosophical." [158]

Charitable people seek truth and strive to be true. We try to be honest, sincere and genuine with others. Brigham Young continues: "I want to say that we are for the truth, the whole truth and nothing but the truth; we are pursuing the path of truth, and by and by we expect to possess a great deal more than we do now." [159]

But the more literal translation of the Revised Version calls for just such a sacrifice for truth's sake here. For what Paul really meant is, as we there read, "Rejoiceth not in

---

[158] Young, Brigham, *Discourses of Brigham Young*, 9:149.
[159] Ibid. 14:196.

unrighteousness, but rejoiceth with the truth," a quality which probably no one English word—and certainly not Sincerity—adequately defines. It includes, perhaps more strictly, the self-restraint which refuses to make capital out of others' faults; the charity *which delights not in exposing the weakness of others, but "covereth all things;" the sincerity of purpose which endeavors to see things as they are, and rejoices to find them better than suspicion feared or calumny denounced.*

"To give real service," wrote Douglas Adams, "you must add something which cannot be bought or measured with money, and that is sincerity and integrity." [160] Love and sincerity are the key to charitable service. When our reality is in complete harmony with our appearance, only then are we truly sincere.

Confucius said that "sincerity and truth are the basis of every virtue." [161] Sincerity has been referred to as "moral truth."

Charity beareth all things. To bear means to support; to sustain the burden of, perhaps including the lightening of others'

---

[160] Source Unknown.
[161] Source Unknown.

The Greatest Thing in the World

burdens; to withstand successfully.

Charity believeth all things. It is not naïve or gullible but is open to all truth. When we have the spiritual gift of a believing heart, all things work together for our good. [162]

Charity hopeth all things. Charity is desire accompanied by anticipation; it is trust. Charitable people have a firm hope in Christ and, although imperfect, they possess an energetic and enthusiastic assurance that eternal life is at the end of the path. The prophet Mormon asked the humble Christians of his day: "What is it that ye shall hope for? Behold I say unto you that ye shall have hope through the atonement of Christ and the power of his resurrection, to be raised unto life eternal." [163] In other words, even though we are imperfect, we have the hope that we are on the right path and that the Lord is pleased with our efforts.

Charity endureth all things. Charity continues, it doesn't give up in the face of adversity. Charity lasts, it doesn't just fade away with the passage of time. Charity remains throughout, it never retreats or runs off at the fear of ridicule, shame, or even death. Nephi tells us that: "If ye shall press forward, feasting upon the word of Christ,

---

[162] See D&C 90:42.
[163] Moroni 7:41.

and endure to the end, behold, thus saith the Father: Ye shall have eternal life." [164]

Charity never faileth. How would you describe something that never fails?

Charity never runs out of power or loses its strength. It is attentive at all times. It is never in short supply. It is never scarce. Charity delights, it never disappoints. Charity is never neglectful. It never abandons or leaves. Charity is helpful. It is useful. It omits nothing and neglects no one. Charity is always enough. The pure love of charity simply never fails!

So much for the analysis of Charity. *Now the business of our lives is to have these things fitted into our characters. That is the supreme work to which we need to address ourselves in this world, to learn* Charity. *Is life not full of opportunities for learning* Charity? *Every man and woman every day has a thousand of them. The world is not a playground; it is a schoolroom. Life is not a holiday, but an education. And*

THE ONE ETERNAL LESSON

for us all is how better we can love.

---

[164] 2 Nephi 31:20.

The Greatest Thing in the World

As a fruit of the Spirit, charity is bestowed by God. We don't develop charity like we develop other skills, like leadership or public speaking. In Paul's words, charity is a "more excellent way." [165] As stated earlier, it comes by and through the Holy Ghost as one of the gifts of God.

We have an obligation and an accountability to serve others and such service is essential to our salvation. It is part of our covenantal commitment as followers of Jesus Christ. [166] But, as we have said, service and charity are not necessarily the same. The LDS Bible Dictionary defines charity as "the highest, noblest, strongest kind of love, not merely affection; the pure love of Christ. It is never used to denote alms or deeds or benevolence, although it may be a prompting motive." [167]

"Perhaps the greatest charity" counseled Marvin J. Ashton, "comes when we are kind to each other, when we don't judge or categorize someone else, when we simply give each other the benefit of the doubt or remain quiet. Charity is accepting someone's differences, weaknesses, and

---

[165] 1 Corinthians 12:31.
[166] See James 2:8; Mosiah 18:8-10.
[167] LDS Bible Dictionary, *Charity*, p.632.

shortcomings; having patience with someone who has let us down; or resisting the impulse to become offended when someone doesn't handle something the way we might have hoped. Charity is refusing to take advantage of another's weakness and being willing to forgive someone who has hurt us. Charity is expecting the best of each other." [168]

How do we fit charity into our characters? It certainly isn't automatic and, though it is a gift, it is a gift which we must seek after and develop. Like any other quality or characteristic, charity, the pure love of God and Christ, is learned.

Mormon reveals the strongest instruction on how to develop charity. He advises us to "pray unto the Father with all the energy of heart, that ye may be filled with this love, which he hath bestowed upon all who are true followers of his Son, Jesus Christ; that ye may become the sons of God; that when he shall appear we shall be like him, for we shall see him as he is; that we may have this hope; that we may be purified even as he is pure." [169]

Charity is the same love that Christ feels toward us. [170] True followers of Christ

---

[168] LDS Bible Dictionary, *Charity*, p.632.
[169] Moroni 7:48.
[170] Ether 12:34.

who "pray with all the energy of heart" are given the surety that they may one day be "filled with this love" known as charity.

So, we have been commanded to pray for this gift, but then what? What are we *willing* to do to instill the pure love of Christ into our characters? Well, let's start with that idea of being willing.

Are we willing to be loving?

Are we willing to do kind things for others?

Are we willing to bear another's burden?

Are we willing to forgive?

Are we willing to mourn with them that mourn and comfort them that stand in need?

Are we willing to be Christ-like Christians?

We all know the saying: "Where there's a will, there's a way." Jesus said: "I am the way." [171] Are we willing to follow His example?

What makes a man a good cricketer? Practice. What makes a man a good artist, a good sculptor, a good musician? Practice. What makes a man a good linguist, a good

---

[171] John 14:6.

stenographer? Practice. What makes a man a good man? Practice. Nothing else. There is nothing capricious about religion. We do not get the soul in different ways, under different laws, from those in which we get the body and the mind. If a man does not exercise his arm he develops no biceps muscle; and if a man does not exercise his soul, he acquires no muscle in his soul, no strength of character, no vigor of moral fibre, no beauty of spiritual growth. Charity *is not a thing of enthusiastic emotion. It is a rich, strong, manly, vigorous expression of the whole round Christian character—the Christlike nature in its fullest development. And the constituents of this great character are only to be built up by*

CEASELESS PRACTICE.

What was Christ doing in the carpenter's shop? Practising. Though perfect, we read that He learned obedience, and grew in wisdom and in favor with God. Do not quarrel, therefore, with your lot in life. Do not complain of its never-ceasing cares, its petty environment, the vexations you have to stand, the small and sordid souls you have to live and work with. Above all, do not resent temptation; do not be perplexed because it seems to thicken round you more and more, and ceases neither for effort nor for agony nor prayer. That is your practice. That is the practice which God appoints you; and it is having its work in making you patient, and humble, and generous, and unselfish, and kind, and courteous. Do not grudge the hand that is moulding the still too shapeless image within you. It is growing more beautiful, though you see it not; and every touch of temptation may add to its perfection. Therefore keep in the midst of life. Do not isolate yourself. Be among men and among things, and among troubles, and difficulties, and obstacles.

You remember Goethe's words: "Talent develops itself in solitude; character in the stream of life." Talent develops itself in solitude—the talent of prayer, of faith, of meditation, of seeing the unseen; character grows in the stream of the world's life. That chiefly is where men are to learn charity.

It has been said that charity is a condition of the heart. It is more than what we do, more than what our outward actions indicate. Charity is what compels us to perform those outward actions in the first place. It is the tenderhearted, compassionate feelings in the depth of our souls that prompt us to act, that do not allow us to "see another's lack and … not share." [172]

The closer we come to our Eternal Father the more we desire to love and serve Him. Like Lehi, once we partake of the fruit of God's love, we will desire to share that experience with others. That is the mission and purpose of the Church and that is also our mission and our purpose. In this sense charity becomes, not just a *condition* of the heart, but also a *conditioning* of the heart. Charity is something we must learn.

"As we learn," advises Aileen Clyde, "we are capable of being kind, without envy, not easily provoked, rejoicing in truth, bearing, believing, hoping, enduring all things. Charity comes to us as we move from grace to grace as we build precept on precept.

"Charity develops in us as we see ourselves moving in our lives from a 'what's in it for me' kind of love, to the love of family and friends and blessedly beyond that to an awareness of our Lord's unconditional love for us that tells us of our divine kinship with one another and with Him. Such love, or charity, does not spring whole and steady in most lives, but it can come as we learn and grow and reach for ways to know God's

---

[172] LDS Hymns, p. 219.

love." [173]

How? Now, how? To make it easier, I have named a few of the elements of charity. *But these are only elements.* Charity *itself can never be defined. Light is a something more than the sum of its ingredients—a glowing, dazzling, tremulous ether. And* Charity *is something more than all its elements—a palpitating, quivering, sensitive, living thing. By synthesis of all the colors, men can make whiteness, they cannot make light. By synthesis of all the virtues, men can make virtue, they cannot make* Charity. *How then are we to have this transcendent living whole conveyed into our souls? We brace our wills to secure it. We try to copy those who have it. We lay down rules about it. We watch. We pray. But these things alone will not bring* Charity *into our nature.* Charity *is an effect. And only as we fulfill the right condition can we have the effect produced. Shall I tell you what the cause is?*

The Apostle John wrote: "God is love; and he that dwelleth in love dwelleth in God, and God in him." [174] Love is a

---

[173] Clyde, Aileen H., General Relief Society Meeting, Sept. 24, 1994.
[174] 1 John 4:16.

foundational part of the gospel. God-like love originates with and emanates from God.

The essential elements of the gospel of Jesus Christ are:

1. Love for God and
2. Love for one another.

When we are baptized as members of the Church of Jesus Christ, we covenant to be Christians. This covenant is an agreement and a promise to love. We can only truly love others as we learn and practice charity. Joseph Smith stated: "Love is one of the chief characteristics of Deity, and ought to be manifested by those who aspire to be the sons of God." [175]

LOVE FOR GOD

Our love for God will grow as we become more aware of His goodness and mercy toward us and as we begin to "acknowledge his hand in all things." [176] Ezra Taft Benson observed that "to love God with all your heart, soul, mind, and strength is all-consuming and all-encompassing …. The

---

[175] Smith, Joseph, *Teachings of the Prophet Joseph Smith*, p. 174.
[176] D&C 59:21.

breadth, depth, and height of this love of God extend into every facet of one's life. Our desires, be they spiritual or temporal, should be rooted in a love of the Lord." [177]

As we feel the weight of sin lifted, the burden of our guilt removed, the bitterness of loss and the hostility of life softened and smoothed over, we will, like Ammon, wish to "give thanks to his holy name, for he doth work righteousness forever." [178] When charity fills our hearts, we will not even be able to express the great love that we feel for our Father.

"Behold," wrote Ammon, "I cannot say the smallest part which I feel." [179]

LOVE FOR HUMANITY

Those who come unto Christ become like Christ. We become partakers of His divine nature. We begin to love as He loves.

In an earlier chapter, I quoted the prophet Joseph Smith who said: "The nearer we get to our Heavenly Father, the more we are disposed to look with compassion on perishing souls; we feel that we want to take

---

[177] Benson, Ezra Taft, *Teachings of Ezra Taft Benson*, p. 349.
[178] Alma 26:8.
[179] Ibid. vs. 16.

them upon our shoulders, and cast their sins behind our backs." [180]

As we become filled with the pure love of God, we serve God and others out of proper motives. Our good deeds and acts of kindness become richer, deeper and more genuine when grounded in feelings of charity. The apostle Paul and the prophet Mormon both wrote of charity as the greatest of all the fruits of the Spirit and as the one that will last forever. [181]

Disciples of Christ, or members of the Church of Jesus Christ, should be bonded together in charity "which is the bond of perfectness and peace." [182] Joseph Smith further taught that "there is a love from God that should be exercised toward those of our faith, who walk uprightly, which is peculiar to itself, but it is without prejudice; it also gives scope to the mind, which enables us to conduct ourselves with greater liberality towards all that are not of our faith, than what they exercise towards one another. These principles approximate nearer to the mind of God, because it is like God, or Godlike." [183]

---

[180] Smith, Joseph, *Teachings of the Prophet Joseph Smith*, pp. 240, 41.
[181] See 1 Corinthians 13:1-13 and Moroni 7:45-48.
[182] D&C 88:125.
[183] Ibid. p. 147.

This bond, this expression of love toward others, should also be extended without limitation to everyone outside the fold of the Church. The prophet continued: "A man filled with the love of God is not content with blessing his family alone, but ranges through the whole world, anxious to bless the whole human race." [184]

Our love for God is resolutely interrelated to our love for each other. We know from the restored gospel that when we are in the service of our fellow beings we are only in the service of our God. [185] Serving others is inseparably connected to salvation. In fact, to retain "a remission of your sins from day to day, that ye may walk guiltless before God—I would that ye should impart of your substance to the poor, every man according to that which he hath, such as feeding the hungry, clothing the naked, visiting the sick and administering to their relief, both spiritually and temporally, according to their wants." [186] Simply stated, service is essential to salvation.

We all know that we can serve others without loving them, but that we cannot love

---

[184] Smith, Joseph, *Teachings of the Prophet Joseph Smith*, p. 174.
[185] Mosiah 2:17.
[186] Mosiah 4:26.

them, not, at least, with the pure love of Christ, without serving them. Charity is a gift of the Spirit. It influences, inspires and impels us to greater goodness. It prompts, persuades and activates us toward greater service and compassion for others.

"The final and crowning virtue of the divine character," explains President Ezra Taft Benson "is charity, or the pure love of Christ. If we would truly seek to be more like our Savior and Master, learning to love as He loves should be our highest goal.... The world today speaks a great deal about love, and it is sought for by many. But the pure love of Christ differs greatly from what the world thinks of love. Charity never seeks selfish gratification. The pure love of Christ seeks only the eternal growth and joy of others." [187]

If you turn to the Revised Version of the First Epistle of John you find these words: "We love because He first loved us." "We love," not "We love Him." That is the way the old version has it, and it is quite wrong. "We love—because He first loved us." Look at that word "because." It is the cause of which I have spoken. "Because He first loved

---

[187] Benson, Ezra Taft, *Teachings of Ezra Taft Benson*, p. 275.

us," the effect follows that we love, we love Him, we love all men. We cannot help it. Because He loved us, we love, we love everybody. Our heart is slowly changed. Contemplate the love of Christ, and you will love. Stand before that mirror, reflect Christ's character, and you will be changed into the same image from tenderness to tenderness. There is no other way. You cannot love to order. You can only look at the lovely object, and fall in love with it, and grow into likeness to it. And so look at this Perfect Character, this Perfect Life. Look at

THE GREAT SACRIFICE

as He laid down Himself, all through life, and upon the Cross of Calvary; and you must love Him. And loving Him, you must become like Him. Love begets love. It is a process of induction. Put a piece of iron in the presence of an electrified body, and that piece of iron for a time becomes electrified. It is changed into a temporary magnet in the mere presence of a permanent magnet, and as long as you leave the two side by side, they are both magnets alike. Remain side by side with Him who loved us, and

GAVE HIMSELF FOR US,

and you, too, will become a permanent magnet, a permanently attractive force; and like Him you will draw all men unto you, like Him you will be drawn unto all men. That is the inevitable effect of Charity. Any man who fulfills that cause must have that effect produced in him.

Elder C. Max Caldwell explains that: "Through His compliance with the severe requirements of the atonement, the Savior offered the ultimate expression of love. And by permitting His Son to make such a selfless and suffering sacrifice, the Father provided us with an ultimate expression of His love as His gift to the rest of His children." [188]

"How deeply do we love Him?" asks Elder Caldwell. "Does our love depend on favorable environments? Is it diminished or strengthened by our experiences? Is our love for Him evident by our behavior and our attitude? Charity, or love for Christ, sustains us in every need and influences us in every decision." [189]

Try to give up the idea that religion

---

[188] Caldwell, C. Max, LDS Church News, October 10, 1992.
[189] Ibid.

comes to us by chance, or by mystery, or by caprice. It comes to us by natural law, or by supernatural law, for all law is Divine.

If we think our religion is something other than love, we are wrong. Joseph Smith taught us that: "To be justified before God we must love one another." [190] True religion is charity, it is love in action.

Saint Augustine has said that "God loves each of us as though there were only one of us." [191]

Edward Irving went to see a dying boy once, and when he entered the room he just put his hand on the sufferer's head, and said, "My boy, God loves you," and went away. The boy started from his bed, and called out to the people in the house,

"God loves me! God loves me!"

One word! It changed that boy. The sense that God loved him overpowered him, melted him down, and began the creating of a new heart in him.

"Something wonderful happens," explains John Bytheway, "when we really know, without a doubt, that God loves us—

---

[190] Smith, Joseph, History of the Church, 2:229.
[191] Source Unknown.

our questions completely change. Instead of asking, 'Why did this happen to me?' or 'Why doesn't God care about me?' we say, 'Well, I know God loves me; I know that. So what can I learn from this experience?'" [192]

God's love is personal. He knows us individually. He loves us personally, not because of who we are, but because of who He is. God is love.

And that is how the love of God melts down the unlovely heart in man, and begets in him the new creature, who is patient and humble and gentle and unselfish. And there is no other way to get it. There is no mystery about it. We love others, we love everybody, we love our enemies, because He first loved us.

Charity is the prime directive. It is the new commandment. "A new commandment I give unto you, That ye love one another; as I have loved you, that ye also love one another. By this shall all men know that ye are my disciples, if ye have love one to another." [193]

No principle in all eternity is greater. The single law to love encompasses all the other laws, rules and commandments in the

---

[192] Bytheway, John, LDS Living.
[193] John 13: 34, 35.

gospel of Jesus Christ. Possessing and acting with charity will make us more Christ-like than any other principle.

If, as Saint Augustine said, God loves each of us as thought there were only one of us, then isn't that also how we should love each other? Christ taught His followers that His Father's kingdom would be inherited by those who had fed the hungry, clothed the naked, and visited the sick or in prison. [194]

To better cultivate charity, William S. Evans, the director of community relations for the Church Public Affairs Department, recommends that we:

"Begin in our neighborhoods and communities, in our wards or branches, among our family members and acquaintances.

"Find service opportunities that fill a need or that match our interests, talents, or hobbies.

"Try helping in the schools, supporting the arts, improving the environment, or serving the handicapped, the elderly, or the disadvantaged." [195]

Cultivating charity, loving God and others, including our enemies, is the one trait above all others that characterizes the Savior.

---

[194] See Matthew 25: 34-40.
[195] Evans, William S., Ensign, June 1990, p. 78.

"The Lord God hath given a commandment" wrote the prophet Nephi, "that all men should have charity, which charity is love. And except they should have charity they were nothing." [196]

The core of the gospel of Jesus Christ is charity. Charity offers us a perfect brightness of hope. Charity qualifies us to be in the presence of God with our eternal family. Charity provides us with the assurance that God lives, that Jesus Christ is our Savior and that Their love for us truly never fails.

If you want to be like God, learn charity.

---

[196] 2 Nephi 26:30.

The Greatest Thing in the World

Chapter Four

THE DEFENCE

Of all the magnificent characteristics of humanity, the highest and most holy of all is charity. Charity has been described as the principle fabric through which all of the other qualities and characteristics weave to create a perfect tapestry of life. Beyond all the attributes of godliness, charity is the one we should most deeply desire.

When we have woven charity into the fabric of our personalities, we will discover a tapestry of life filled with faith, abiding and abounding in hope and laden with a love for God and for all of humanity. The pattern of our life will be purity of heart, spontaneous service seasoned with sincere love, and forgiveness rendered without reservation. Our individual actions and activities will be to lift and to bless, to share with the underprivileged and impoverished, to clothe the naked, feed the hungry, visit the sick and imprisoned, to forgo judgment and to do it all, not for our own glory or praise, but for the praise and glory of God.

This is the charity that "never faileth." Far more than love, it is perfect, everlasting, pure love. Charity is so centered in Christ-like service and behavior that its sole ambition is the eternal welfare of humanity.[197]

Now I have a closing sentence or two to add about Paul's reason for singling out charity *as the supreme possession.*

It is a very remarkable reason. In a single word it is this: it lasts. "Charity," urges Paul, "never faileth." Then he begins again one of his marvelous lists of the great things of the day, and exposes them one by one. He runs over the things that men thought were going to last, and shows that they are all fleeting, temporary, passing away.

"Whether there be prophecies, they shall be done away." It was the mother's

---

[197] See 2 Nephi 26:30; Moroni 7:47; 8:25-26.

The Greatest Thing in the World

ambition for her boy in those days that he should become a prophet. For hundreds of years God had never spoken by means of any prophet, and at that time the prophet was greater than the king. Men waited wistfully for another messenger to come, and hung upon his lips when he appeared, as upon the very voice of God. Paul says, "Whether there be prophecies, they shall fail." The Bible is full of prophecies. One by one they have "failed"; that is, having been fulfilled, their work is finished; they have nothing more to do now in the world except to feed a devout man's faith.

Then Paul talks about tongues. That was another thing that was greatly coveted. "Whether there be tongues, they shall cease." As we all know, many many centuries have passed since tongues have been known in this world. They have ceased. Take it in any sense you like. Take it, for illustration merely, as languages in general—a sense which was not in Paul's mind at all, and which though it cannot give us the specific lesson, will point the general truth. Consider the words in which these chapters were written—Greek. It has gone. Take the Latin—the other great tongue of those days. It ceased long ago. Look at the Indian language. It is ceasing. The language of Wales, of Ireland, of the Scottish Highlands is dying before our eyes. The most popular book in the English tongue at the present time, except the Bible, is one of Dickens' works, his Pickwick Papers. It is largely written in the language of London street-life; and experts assure us that in fifty years it will be unintelligible to the average English reader.

Both Paul and Mormon tell us that charity lasts forever. It never fails. [198] Other gifts will render themselves useless; prophecy, tongues, knowledge will at some point become useless functions. When this time comes, charity, the pure love of Christ, will still be in full operational mode. When other gifts are done away with, the gift of Charity will still burn bright in the hearts of the children of God because "when that which is perfect is come" [199] those who are filled with charity will become like Christ who is the supreme personification of pure love.

Then Paul goes farther, and with even greater boldness adds, "Whether there be knowledge, it shall be done away." The wisdom of the ancients, where is it? It is

---

[198] 1 Corinthians 13:8; Moroni 7: 46, 47.
[199] 1 Corinthians 13:10.

The Greatest Thing in the World

wholly gone. A schoolboy to-day knows more than Sir Isaac Newton knew; his knowledge has vanished away. You put yesterday's newspaper in the fire: its knowledge has vanished away. You buy the old editions of the great encyclopædias for a few cents: their knowledge has vanished away. Look how the coach has been superseded by the use of steam. Look how electricity has superseded that, and swept a hundred almost new inventions into oblivion. One of the greatest living authorities, Sir William Thompson, said in Scotland, at a meeting at which I was present, "The steam-engine is passing away." "Whether there be knowledge, it shall vanish away." At every workshop you will see, in the back yard, a heap of old iron, a few wheels, a few levers, a few cranks, broken and eaten with rust. Twenty years ago that was the pride of the city. Men flocked in from the country to see the great invention; now it is superseded, its day is done. And all the boasted science and philosophy of this day will soon be old.

In my time, in the university of Edinburgh, the greatest figure in the faculty was Sir James Simpson, the discoverer of chloroform. Recently his successor and nephew, Professor Simpson, was asked by the librarian of the University to go to the library and pick out the books on his subject (midwifery) that were no longer needed. His reply to the librarian was this:

"Take every text-book that is more than ten years old and put it down in the cellar."

Sir James Simpson was a great authority only a few years ago: men came from all parts of the earth to consult him; and almost the whole teaching of that time is consigned by the science of to-day to oblivion. And in every branch of science it is the same. "Now we know in part. We see through a glass darkly." Knowledge does not last.

In the eternal world we will know the innate inspirations, the shrouded sentiments, the silent thoughts and unspoken syllables of each other. It has been said that we will be like transparent crystal and all the beautiful unspoken words and utterances will all be understood. We will know each other's heart and mind. As Paul informs us: "Now we see through a glass, darkly; but then face to face: now I know in part, but then shall I know even as also I am known." [200]

---

[200] 1 Corinthians 13:12.

The Greatest Thing in the World

Can you tell me anything that is going to last? Many things Paul did not condescend to name. He did not mention money, fortune, fame; but he picked out the great things of his time, the things the best men thought had something in them, and brushed them peremptorily aside. Paul had no charge against these things in themselves. All he said about them was that they would not last. They were great things, but not supreme things. There were things beyond them. What we are stretches past what we do, beyond what we possess. Many things that men denounce as sins are not sins; but they are temporary. And that is a favorite argument of the New Testament. John says of the world, not that it is wrong, but simply that it "passeth away." There is a great deal in the world that is delightful and beautiful; there is a great deal in it that is great and engrossing; but

IT WILL NOT LAST.

All that is in the world, the lust of the eye, the lust of the flesh, and the pride of life, are but for a little while. Love not the world therefore. Nothing that it contains is worth the life and consecration of an immortal soul. The immortal soul must give itself to something that is immortal. And the only immortal things are these: "Now abideth faith, hope, charity, *but the greatest of these is* charity.*"*

Some think the time may come when two of these three things will also pass away—faith into sight, hope into fruition. Paul does not say so. We know but little now about the conditions of the life that is to come. But what is certain is that Charity *must last. God, the Eternal God, is Love. Covet, therefore, that everlasting gift, that one thing which it is certain is going to stand, that one coinage which will be current in the Universe when all the other coinages of all the nations of the world shall be useless and unhonored. You will give yourselves to many things, give yourself first to* Charity. *Hold things in their proportion. Let at least the first great object of our lives be to achieve the character defended in these words, the character—and it is the character of Christ—which is built round* Charity.

Charity is "the greatest of all." [201] We achieve our highest potential in this world through kindness and charity toward others and through love toward God. Jesus Christ demonstrated for us the doctrine of service.

---

[201] Moroni 7:46.

He declared the divine law of doing good to others, even to our enemies. Charity is the crowning virtue of a celestial character and, if we truly desire to be like our Savior, we will learn to love as He did.

Our highest goal should be to develop a love for people. Our hearts should go out to others in a desire to lift them up, to build them up, to point them up to a better life, a higher state of being and, eventually, to exaltation in the eternal realms of the Father.

I have said this thing is eternal. Did you ever notice how continually John associates love and faith with eternal life? I was not told when I was a boy that "God so loved the world that He gave His only-begotten Son, that whosoever believeth in Him should have everlasting life." What I was told, I remember, was, that God so loved the world that, if I trusted in Him, I was to have a thing called peace, or I was to have rest, or I was to have joy, or I was to have safety. But I had to find out for myself that whosoever trusteth in Him—that is, whosoever loveth Him, for trust is only the avenue to Love—hath

EVERLASTING LIFE.

The Greatest Thing in the World

Charity is the foundation of true worship. It puts heart into our adoration, soul into our service and spirit into our existence. Charity conquers conceit, overpowers pride and vanquishes avarice and greed. It fosters feelings of love for all and fulfills the second law of loving our neighbor. In the world in which we live, love of neighbor finds expression in Christian acts of charity and kindness to those in need in an environment in which all humanity across the earth is seen as our neighbor.

The Gospel offers a man a life. Never offer a man a thimbleful of Gospel. Do not offer them merely joy, or merely peace, or merely rest, or merely safety; tell them how Christ came to give men a more abundant life than they have, a life abundant in charity, *and therefore abundant in salvation for themselves, and large in enterprise for the alleviation and redemption of the world. Then only can the Gospel take hold of the whole of a man, body, soul and spirit, and give to each part of his nature its exercise and reward. Many of the current Gospels are addressed only to a part of man's nature. They offer peace, not life; faith, not* Charity; *justification, not regeneration. And men slip back again from such religion because it has never really held them. Their nature was not all in it. It offered no deeper and gladder life-current than the life that was lived before. Surely it stands to reason that only a fuller love can compete with the love of the world.*

"We then that are strong," advises the apostle Paul, "ought to bear the infirmities of the weak and," he adds, "not to please ourselves." [202] But the true purpose of charity is not simply to motivate us to be nicer to each other, although that is a beautiful side effect. The definitive intention of charity is to craft us to become like Christ. God will bestow upon all who are "true followers of his Son, Jesus Christ; that ye may become the sons of God; that when he shall appear we shall be like him… that we may be purified even as he is pure." [203]

And though we must qualify as "true followers of his son," we cannot, on our own at least, develop complete and enduring charity toward God and humanity. Charity, in its absolute and perfect denotation, is "bestowed" on Jesus' true followers. Yes, our own heart-felt compassion for the plight, the needs, the suffering of others is an important indication of our aspiration to be like the

---

[202] Romans 15:1.
[203] Moroni 7:48.

Savior. We should and we must reach out to others. But even then, the source of charity, like all the gifts of the Atonement, is the grace of God: "I prayed unto the Lord that he would give unto the Gentiles grace, that they might have charity." [204]

To love abundantly is to live abundantly, and to love forever is to live forever. Hence, eternal life is inextricably bound up with love. We want to live forever for the same reason that we want to live to-morrow. Why do we want to live to-morrow? Is it because there is some one who loves you, and whom you want to see to-morrow, and be with, and love back? There is no other reason why we should live on than that we love and are beloved. It is when a man has no one to love him that he commits suicide. So long as he has friends, those who love him and whom he loves, he will live, because to live is to love. Be it but the love of a dog, it will keep him in life; but let that go, he has no contact with life, no reason to live. He dies by his own hand.

Eternal life also is to know God, and God is love. This is Christ's own definition. Ponder it. "This is life eternal, that they

---

[204] Ether 12:36.

might know Thee the only true God, and Jesus Christ whom Thou hast sent." Love must be eternal. It is what God is. On the last analysis, then, love is life. Charity *never faileth, and life never faileth, so long as there is love. That is the philosophy of what Paul is showing us; the reason why in the nature of things* Charity *should be the supreme thing— because it is going to last; because in the nature of things it is an Eternal Life. It is a thing that we are living now, not that we get when we die; that we shall have a poor chance of getting when we die unless we are living now.*

NO WORSE FATE

can befall a man in this world than to live and grow old alone, unloving and unloved. To be lost is to live in an unregenerate condition, loveless and unloved; and to be saved is to love; and he that dwelleth in love dwelleth already in God. For God is Love.

I wonder if it is humanly possible to completely comprehend the gift of charity, the pure love of Christ. It seems an overwhelming, if not impossible, task. Charity must be an absolute and total submission of both the mind and the heart in such an utterly selfless sense of serving the souls of humanity with only the sincerest intent.

When my father was serving his first full-time mission for the Church, he contemplated the following verse of scripture found in Matthew: "Let your light so shine before men, that they may see your good works, and glorify your Father which is in heaven." [205]

"How can I serve," he wrote home to his mother, "in such a way that when others see me, they don't feel to thank me but instead to glorify their Father in heaven?"

That is one of the grand elements of true charity. We cannot and must not expect admiration, appreciation, gratefulness or any similar manner of reward or recognition as the normal after-effect of blessing the life of another. Our minds must be void of vanity and the intent of our heart must be pure. To Titus, Paul wrote: "Unto the pure all things are pure." [206] Pure intent is part and parcel to charity.

Now I have all but finished. How many of you will join me in reading this chapter [of 1st Corinthians 13] *once a week*

---
[205] Matthew 5:16.
[206] Titus 1:5.

for the next three months? A man did that once and it changed his whole life. Will you do it? It is for the greatest thing in the world. You might begin by reading it every day, especially the verses which describe the perfect character. "Charity *suffereth long, and is kind;* charity *envieth not;* charity *vaunteth not itself."* *Get these ingredients into your life. Then everything that you do is eternal. It is worth doing. It is worth giving time to.*

No man can become a saint in his sleep; and to fulfill the condition required demands a certain amount of prayer and meditation and time, just as improvement in any direction, bodily or mental, requires preparation and care. Address yourselves to that one thing; at any cost have this transcendent character exchanged for yours.

No one is an island. None of us stand alone. We should build, strengthen and encourage each other. When an ill woman touched the hem of Jesus' garment, He felt strength go out of him. His strength strengthened the woman. We should seek to do the same.

- Cultivate the art of complimenting others.
- Seek for occasions to strengthen

- someone.
- Initiate opportunities to encourage others.

As followers of Jesus Christ we have a divinely designated responsibility to bear one another's burdens, to strengthen, lift, encourage and build up one another.

You will find as you look back upon your life that the moments that stand out, the moments when you have really lived, are the moments when you have done things in a spirit of love. As memory scans the past, above and beyond all the transitory pleasures of life, there leap forward those supreme hours when you have been enabled to do unnoticed kindnesses to those round about you, things too trifling to speak about, but which you feel have entered into your eternal life. I have seen almost all the beautiful things God has made; I have enjoyed almost every pleasure that He has planned for man; and yet as I look back I see standing out above all the life that has gone four or five short experiences, when the love of God reflected itself in some poor imitation, some small act of charity of mine, and these seem to be the things which alone of all one's life abide. Everything else in all our lives is transitory. Every other good is visionary. But the acts of charity *which no man knows about, or can ever know about—they never fail.*

Charity is the most valuable gift we can receive and the most precious offering we can extend to others. Whether it is through sharing our substance, lightening another's load, or a mere expression of appreciation, to give of ourselves without price or expectation is the essence of charity.

In the Book of Matthew, where the Judgment Day is depicted for us in the imagery of One seated upon a throne and dividing the sheep from the goats, the test of a man then is not, "How have I believed?" but "How have I loved?" The test of religion, the final test of religion, is not religiousness, but Charity. *I say the final test of religion at that great Day is not religiousness, but* Charity; *not what I have done, not what I have believed, not what I have achieved, but how I have discharged the common charities of life.*

Swami Vivekananda tells us that: "Love and charity for the whole human race, that is the test of true religiousness." [207]

---

[207] www.swamivivekanandaquotes.com.

It is the Son of Man before whom the nations of the world shall be gathered. It is in the presence of Humanity that we shall be charged. And the spectacle itself, the mere sight of it, will silently judge each one. Those will be there whom we have met and helped; or there, the unpitied multitude whom we neglected or despised. No other witness need be summoned.

Joseph Smith pointed out that one of the evidences that "men are unacquainted with the principles of godliness" is when we witness "the contraction of affectionate feelings and lack of charity in the world. The power and glory of godliness is spread out on a broad principle to throw out the mantle of charity." We cannot withhold kindness, caring or concern from anyone. We cannot forbear forgiveness, even to the unrepentant. "God does not look on sin with allowance," continued the Prophet Joseph, "but when men have sinned, there must be allowance made for them." [208]

Peter told the saints in his day: "Above all things have fervent charity among yourselves, for charity shall cover the

---

[208] Source Unknown.

multitude of sins." [209]

"The words which all of us shall one Day hear sound not of theology, but of life, not of churches and saints but of the hungry and the poor, not of creeds and doctrines, but of shelter and clothing, not of Bibles and prayerbooks but of cups of cold water offered in the name of Christ." [210]

Sins of commission in that lawful indictment are not even referred to. By what we have not done, by sins of omission, we are judged. It could not be otherwise. For the withholding of charity *is the negation of the spirit of Christ, the proof that we never knew Him, that for us He lived in vain. It means that He suggested nothing in all our thoughts, that He inspired nothing in all our lives, that we were not once near enough to Him, to be seized with the spell of His compassion for the world. It means that—*

"I lived for myself, I thought for myself,
For myself, and none beside—
Just as if Jesus had never lived,
As if He had never died."

---

[209] 1 Peter 4:8.
[210] Drummond, Henry, *The Greatest Thing in the World*, Hallmark Edition, 1967. pp. 28, 29.

The Greatest Thing in the World

Thank God the Christianity of today is coming nearer the world's need. Live to help that on. Thank God men know better, by a hair's breadth, what religion is, what God is, who Christ is, where Christ is. Who is Christ? He who fed the hungry, clothed the naked, visited the sick. And where is Christ? Where? "Whoso shall receive a little child in My name receiveth Me." And who are Christ's? "Every one that loveth is born of God."

Charity, then, is the highest virtue, "the end of the commandment." [211] The definitive objective of the gospel of Jesus Christ is to assist us to become as Christ is.

Charity is evidence of the influence of the Holy Ghost in our lives. And charity enables us to endure faithfully to the end. Only the pure love of Christ will move us through this life into the glorious eternal realms of tomorrow.

Christ's love suffereth long and is kind. Christ's love is not puffed up nor easily provoked. Christ's pure love enables Him—and us—to bear all things, believe all things, hope all things, and endure all things. [212]

---

[211] 1 Timothy 1:5.
[212] See Moroni 7:45.

The Lord looks upon the heart. It is not the depth of our knowledge, the power of our position, our exquisite talents and abilities, or our overwhelming wealth that will matter in the eternities. Nothing will do more for our salvation or for our damnation than how we feel toward God and toward God's other children.

It is easy to focus on things—on goals, on who's right and who's wrong, on careers and ambitions, on getting ahead in the world and to forget that it is humanity that matters most. The business of God is humanity. "This is my work and my glory" He declared, "to bring to pass the immortality and eternal life of man." [213] And humanity must be our business as well.

We must pray for charity. We must plead for it. We must ask for it with all the energy of our hearts. Charity comes from the Lord, the source of all good. If we trust in God and yield our hearts unto him, [214] then may we say as did the apostle Paul, "that neither death, nor life, nor angels, nor principalities, nor powers, nor things present, nor things to come, nor height, nor depth, nor any other creature, shall be able to separate us from the love of God, which is in Christ Jesus

---

[213] Moses 1:39.
[214] See Helaman 3:35.

our Lord." [215]

With the help of the Savior, who is the author and distributor of charity, may we increase our capacity to love.

---

[215] Romans 8:38, 39.

The Greatest Thing in the World

DRUMMOND'S ORIGINAL TEXT

LOVE:

THE GREATEST THING IN THE WORLD.

Every one has asked himself the great question of antiquity as of the modern world: What is the summum bonum—the supreme good? You have life before you. Once only you can live it. What is the noblest object of desire, the supreme gift to covet?

The Greatest Thing in the World

We have been accustomed to be told that the greatest thing in the religious world is Faith. That great word has been the key-note for centuries of the popular religion; and we have easily learned to look upon it as the greatest thing in the world. Well, we are wrong. If we have been told that, we may miss the mark. In the 13th chapter of I Corinthians, Paul takes us to

CHRISTIANITY AT ITS SOURCE;

and there we see, "The greatest of these is love."

It is not an oversight. Paul was speaking of faith just a moment before. He says, "If I have all faith, so that I can remove mountains, and have not love, I am nothing." So far from forgetting, he deliberately contrasts them, "Now abideth Faith, Hope, Love," and without a moment's hesitation the decision falls, "The greatest of these is Love."

And it is not prejudice. A man is apt to recommend to others his own strong point. Love was not Paul's strong point. The observing student can detect a beautiful tenderness growing and ripening all through his character as Paul gets old; but the hand that wrote, "The greatest of these is love," when we meet it first, is stained with blood.

Nor is this letter to the Corinthians peculiar in singling out love as the summum bonum. The masterpieces of Christianity are agreed about it. Peter says, "Above all things have fervent love among yourselves." Above all things. And John goes farther, "God is love."

You remember the profound remark which Paul makes elsewhere, "Love is the fulfilling of the law." Did you ever think what he meant by that?

In those days men were working the passage to Heaven by keeping the Ten Commandments, and the hundred and ten other commandments which they had manufactured out of them. Christ came and said, "I will show you a more simple way. If you do one thing, you will do these hundred and ten things, without ever thinking about them. If you love, you will unconsciously fulfill the whole law."

You can readily see for yourselves how that must be so. Take any of the commandments. "Thou shalt have no other gods before Me." If a man love God, you will not require to tell him that. Love is the fulfilling of that law. "Take not His name in vain." Would he ever dream of taking His name in vain if he loved him? "Remember the

Sabbath day to keep it holy." Would he not be too glad to have one day in seven to dedicate more exclusively to the object of his affection? Love would fulfill all these laws regarding God.

And so, if he loved man, you would never think of telling him to honor his father and mother. He could not do anything else. It would be preposterous to tell him not to kill. You could only insult him if you suggested that he should not steal—how could he steal from those he loved? It would be superfluous to beg him not to bear false witness against his neighbor. If he loved him it would be the last thing he would do. And you would never dream of urging him not to covet what his neighbors had. He would rather they possessed it than himself. In this way "Love is the fulfilling of the law." It is the rule for fulfilling all rules, the new commandment for keeping all the old commandments, Christ's one

SECRET OF THE CHRISTIAN LIFE.

Now Paul has learned that; and in this noble eulogy he has given us the most wonderful and original account extant of the summum bonum. We may divide it into three parts. In the beginning of the short chapter we have

The Greatest Thing in the World

Love contrasted; in the heart of it, we have Love analyzed; toward the end, we have Love defended as the supreme gift.

The Greatest Thing in the World

I. THE CONTRAST.

Paul begins by contrasting Love with other things that men in those days thought much of. I shall not attempt to go over these things in detail. Their inferiority is already obvious.

He contrasts it with eloquence. And what a noble gift it is, the power of playing upon the souls and wills of men, and rousing them to lofty purposes and holy deeds! Paul says, "If I speak with the tongues of men and of angels, and have not love, I am become sounding brass, or a tinkling cymbal." We all know why.

We have all felt the brazenness of words without emotion, the hollowness, the unaccountable unpersuasiveness, of eloquence behind which lies no Love.

He contrasts it with prophecy. He contrasts it with mysteries. He contrasts it with faith. He contrasts it with charity. Why is Love greater than faith? Because the end is greater than the means. And why is it greater than charity? Because the whole is greater than the part.

Love is greater than faith, because the end is greater than the means. What is the use of having faith? It is to connect the soul with God. And what is the object of connecting man with God? That he may become like God. But God is Love. Hence Faith, the means, is in order to Love, the end. Love, therefore, obviously is greater than faith. "If I have all faith, so as to remove mountains, but have not love, I am nothing."

It is greater than charity, again, because the whole is greater than a part. Charity is only a little bit of Love, one of the innumerable avenues of Love, and there may even be, and there is, a great deal of charity without Love. It is a very easy thing to toss a copper to a beggar on the street; it is generally an easier thing than not to do it. Yet Love is just as often in the withholding. We purchase relief from the sympathetic feelings roused by the spectacle of misery, at the copper's cost. It is too cheap—too cheap for us, and often too dear for the beggar. If we really loved him we would either do more for him, or less. Hence, "If I bestow all my goods to feed the poor, but have not love it profiteth me nothing."

Then Paul contrasts it with sacrifice and martyrdom: "If I give my body to be burned, but have not love, it profiteth me nothing." Missionaries can take nothing greater to the heathen world than the impress and reflection of the Love of God upon their own character. That is the universal language. It will take them years to speak in

Chinese, or in the dialects of India. From the day they land, that language of Love, understood by all, will be pouring forth its unconscious eloquence.

It is the man who is the missionary, it is not his words. His character is his message. In the heart of Africa, among the great Lakes, I have come across black men and women who remembered the only white man they ever saw before—David Livingstone; and as you cross his footsteps in that dark continent,

MEN'S FACES LIGHT UP

as they speak of the kind doctor who passed there years ago. They could not understand him; but they felt the love that beat in his heart. They knew that it was love, although he spoke no word.

Take into your sphere of labor, where you also mean to lay down your life, that simple charm, and your lifework must succeed. You can take nothing greater, you need take nothing less. You may take every accomplishment; you may be braced for every sacrifice; but if you give your body to be burned, and have not Love, it will profit you and the cause of Christ nothing.

The Greatest Thing in the World

II. THE ANALYSIS.

After contrasting Love with these things, Paul, in three verses, very short, gives us an amazing analysis of what this supreme thing is.

I ask you to look at it. It is a compound thing, he tells us. It is like light. As you have seen a man of science take a beam of light and pass it through a crystal prism, as you have seen it come out on the other side of the prism broken up into its component colors—red, and blue, and yellow, and violet, and orange, and all the colors of the rainbow—so Paul passes this thing, Love, through the magnificent prism of his inspired intellect, and it comes out on the other side broken up into its elements.

In these few words we have what one might call

THE SPECTRUM OF LOVE,

the analysis of Love. Will you observe what its elements are? Will you notice that they have common names; that they are virtues which we hear about every day; that they are things which can be practised by every man in every place in life; and how, by a multitude of small things and ordinary virtues, the supreme thing, the summum bonum, is made up?

The Spectrum of Love has nine ingredients:

Patience	"Love suffereth long."
Kindness	"And is kind."
Generosity	"Love envieth not."
Humility	"Love vaunteth not itself, is not puffed up."
Courtesy	"Doth not behave itself unseemly."
Unselfishness	"Seeketh not its own."
Good temper	"Is not provoked."
Guilelessness	"Taketh not account of evil."
Sincerity	"Rejoiceth not in unrighteousness, but rejoiceth with the truth."

Patience; kindness; generosity; humility; courtesy; unselfishness; good temper; guilelessness; sincerity—these make up the supreme gift, the stature of the perfect man.

You will observe that all are in relation to men, in relation to life, in relation to the known to-day and the near to-morrow, and not to the unknown eternity. We hear much of love to God; Christ spoke much of love to man. We make a great deal of peace with heaven; Christ made much of peace on earth. Religion is not a strange or added thing, but the inspiration of the secular life, the breathing of an eternal spirit through this temporal world. The supreme thing, in short, is not a thing at all, but the giving of a further finish to the multitudinous words and acts which make up the sum of every common day.

Patience. This is the normal attitude of love; Love passive, Love waiting to begin; not in a hurry; calm; ready to do its work when the summons comes, but meantime wearing the ornament of a meek and quiet spirit. Love suffers long; beareth all things; believeth all things; hopeth all things. For Love understands, and therefore waits.

Kindness. Love active. Have you ever noticed how much of Christ's life was spent in doing kind things—in merely doing kind things? Run over it with that in view, and you will find that He spent a great proportion of His time simply in making people happy, in

DOING GOOD TURNS

to people. There is only one thing greater than happiness in the world, and that is holiness; and it is not in our keeping; but what God has put in our power is the happiness of those about us, and that is largely to be secured by our being kind to them.

"The greatest thing," says some one, "a man can do for his Heavenly Father is to be kind to some of His other children." I wonder why it is that we are not all kinder than we are? How much the world needs it! How easily it is done! How instantaneously it acts! How infallibly it is remembered! How superabundantly it pays itself back—for there is no debtor in the world so honorable, so superbly honorable, as Love. "Love never faileth." Love is success, Love is happiness, Love is life. "Love," I say with Browning, "is energy of life."

"For life, with all it yields of joy or woe
And hope and fear,
Is just our chance o' the prize of learning love,
How love might be, hath been indeed, and is."

Where Love is, God is. He that dwelleth in Love dwelleth in God. God is Love. Therefore love. Without distinction, without calculation, without procrastination, love. Lavish it upon the poor, where it is very easy; especially upon the rich, who often need it most; most of all upon our equals, where it is very difficult, and for whom perhaps we each do least of all. There is a difference between trying to please and giving pleasure. Give pleasure. Lose no chance of giving pleasure; for that is the ceaseless and anonymous triumph of a truly loving spirit. "I shall pass through this world but once. Any good thing, therefore, that I can do, or any kindness that I can show to any human being, let me do it now. Let me not defer it or neglect it, for I shall not pass this way again."

Generosity. "Love envieth not." This is love in competition with others. Whenever you attempt a good work you will find other men doing the same kind of work, and probably doing it better. Envy them not. Envy is a feeling of ill-will to those who are in the same line as ourselves, a spirit of covetousness and detraction. How little Christian work even is a protection against un-Christian feeling! That most despicable of all the unworthy moods which cloud a Christian's soul assuredly waits for us on the threshold of every work, unless we are fortified with this grace of magnanimity. Only one thing truly need the Christian envy—the large, rich, generous soul which "envieth not."

And then, after having learned all that, you have to learn this further thing, **Humility**—to put a seal upon your lips and forget what you have done. After you have been kind, after Love has stolen forth into the world and done its beautiful work, go back into the shade again and say nothing about it. Love hides even from itself. Love waives even self-satisfaction. "Love vaunteth not itself, is not puffed up." Humility—love hiding.

The fifth ingredient is a somewhat strange one to find in this summum bonum: **Courtesy.** This is Love in society, Love in relation to etiquette. "Love does not behave itself unseemly."

Politeness has been defined as love in trifles. Courtesy is said to be love in little things. And the one secret of politeness is to love.

Love cannot behave itself unseemly. You can put the most untutored persons into the highest society, and if they have a reservoir of Love in their heart they will not behave themselves unseemly. They simply cannot do it. Carlisle said of Robert Burns that there was no truer gentleman in Europe than the ploughman-poet. It was because he loved everything—the mouse, and the daisy, and all the things, great and small, that God had made. So with this simple passport he could mingle with any society, and enter courts and palaces from his little cottage on the banks of the Ayr.

You know the meaning of the word "gentleman." It means a gentle man—a man who does things gently, with love. That is the whole art and mystery of it. The gentle man cannot in the nature of things do an ungentle, an ungentlemanly thing. The ungentle soul, the inconsiderate, unsympathetic nature, cannot do anything else. "Love doth not behave itself unseemly."

Unselfishness. "Love seeketh not her own." Observe: Seeketh not even that which is her own. In Britain the Englishman is devoted, and rightly, to his rights. But there come times when a man may exercise even

THE HIGHER RIGHT

of giving up his rights.

Yet Paul does not summon us to give up our rights. Love strikes much deeper. It would have us not seek them at all, ignore them, eliminate the personal element altogether from our calculations.

It is not hard to give up our rights. They are often eternal. The difficult thing is to give up ourselves. The more difficult thing still is not to seek things for ourselves at all. After we have sought them, bought them, won them, deserved them, we have taken the cream off them for ourselves already. Little cross then to give them up. But not to seek them, to look every man not on his own things, but on the things of others—that is the difficulty. "Seekest thou great things for thyself?" said the prophet; "seek them not." Why? Because there is no greatness in things. Things cannot be great. The only greatness is unselfish love. Even self-denial in itself is nothing, is almost a mistake. Only a great purpose or a mightier love can justify the waste.

It is more difficult, I have said, not to seek our own at all than, having sought it, to give it up. I must take that back. It is only true of a partly selfish heart. Nothing is a hardship to Love, and nothing is hard. I believe that Christ's "yoke" is easy. Christ's yoke is just His way of taking life. And I believe it is an easier way than any other. I believe it is a happier way than any other. The most obvious lesson in Christ's teaching is that there is no happiness in having and getting anything, but only in giving. I repeat, there is no happiness in having or in getting, but only in giving. Half the world is on the wrong scent in pursuit of happiness. They think it consists in having and getting, and in being served by others. It consists in giving, and in serving others. "He that would be great among you," said Christ, "let him serve." He that would be happy, let him remember that there is but one way—"it is more blessed, it is more happy, to give than to receive."

The next ingredient is a very remarkable one: **Good temper**. "Love is not provoked."

Nothing could be more striking than to find this here. We are inclined to look upon bad temper as a very harmless weakness. We speak of it as a mere infirmity of nature, a family failing, a matter of temperament, not a thing to take into very serious account in estimating a man's character. And yet here, right in the heart of this analysis of love, it finds a place; and the Bible again and again returns to condemn it as one of the most destructive elements in human nature.

The peculiarity of ill temper is that it is the vice of the virtuous. It is often the one blot on an otherwise noble character. You know men who are all but perfect, and women who would be entirely perfect, but for an easily ruffled, quick-tempered, or "touchy" disposition. This compatibility of ill temper with high moral character is one of the strangest and saddest problems of ethics. The truth is, there are two great classes of sins—sins of the Body and sins of the Disposition. The Prodigal Son may be taken as a type of the first, the Elder Brother of the second. Now, society has no doubt whatever as to which of these is the worse. Its brand falls, without a challenge, upon the Prodigal. But are we right? We have no balance to weigh one another's sins, and coarser and finer are but human words; but faults in the higher nature may be less venal than those in the lower, and to the eye of Him who is Love, a sin against Love may seem a hundred times more base. No form of vice, not worldliness, not greed of gold, not drunkenness itself, does more to un-Christianize society than evil temper. For embittering life, for breaking up communities, for destroying the most sacred relationships, for devastating homes, for withering up men and women, for taking the bloom of childhood, in short,

FOR SHEER GRATUITOUS MISERY-PRODUCING POWER

this influence stands alone.

Look at the Elder Brother—moral, hard-working, patient, dutiful—let him get all credit for his virtues—look at this man, this baby, sulking outside his own father's door. "He was angry," we read, "and would not go in." Look at the effect upon the father, upon the servants, upon the happiness of the guests. Judge of the effect upon the Prodigal—and how many prodigals are kept out of the Kingdom of God by the unlovely character of those who profess to be inside. Analyze, as a study in Temper, the thunder-cloud itself as it gathers upon the Elder Brother's brow. What is it made of? Jealousy, anger, pride, uncharity, cruelty, self-righteousness, touchiness, doggedness, sullenness—these are the ingredients of this dark and loveless soul. In varying proportions, also, these are the ingredients of all ill temper. Judge if such sins of the disposition are not worse to live in, and for others to live with, than the sins of the body. Did Christ indeed not answer the question Himself when He said, "I say unto you that the publicans and the harlots go into the Kingdom of Heaven before you"? There is really no place in heaven for a disposition like this. A man with such a mood could only make heaven miserable for all the people in it. Except, therefore, such a man be

BORN AGAIN,

he cannot, simply cannot, enter the kingdom of heaven.

You will see then why Temper is significant. It is not in what it is alone, but in what it reveals. This is why I speak of it with such unusual plainness. It is a test for love, a symptom, a revelation of an unloving nature at bottom. It is the intermittent fever which bespeaks unintermittent disease within; the occasional bubble escaping to the surface which betrays some rottenness underneath; a sample of the most hidden products of the soul dropped involuntarily when off one's guard; in a word, the lightning form of a hundred hideous and un-Christian sins. A want of patience, a want of kindness, a want of generosity, a want of courtesy, a want of unselfishness, are all instantaneously symbolized in one flash of Temper.

Hence it is not enough to deal with the Temper. We must go to the source, and change the inmost nature, and the angry humors will die away of themselves. Souls are made sweet not by taking the acid fluids out, but by putting something in—a great Love, a new Spirit, the Spirit of Christ. Christ, the Spirit of Christ, interpenetrating ours, sweetens, purifies, transforms all. This only can eradicate what is wrong, work a chemical change, renovate and regenerate, and rehabilitate the inner man. Will-power does not change men. Time does not change men.

CHRIST DOES.

Therefore, "Let that mind be in you which was also in Christ Jesus."

Some of us have not much time to lose. Remember, once more, that this is a matter of life or death. I cannot help speaking urgently, for myself, for yourselves. "Whoso shall offend one of these little ones, which believe in me, it were better for him that a millstone were hanged about his neck, and that he were drowned in the depth of the sea." That is to say, it is the deliberate verdict of the Lord Jesus that it is better not to live than not to love. It is better not to live than not to love.

Guilelessness and **Sincerity** may be dismissed almost without a word. Guilelessness is the grace for suspicious people. The possession
of it is

THE GREAT SECRET OF PERSONAL INFLUENCE.

You will find, if you think for a

moment, that the people who influence you are people who believe in you. In an atmosphere of suspicion men shrivel up; but in that atmosphere they expand, and find encouragement and educative fellowship.

It is a wonderful thing that here and there in this hard, uncharitable world there should still be left a few rare souls who think no evil. This is the great unworldliness. Love "thinketh no evil," imputes no motive, sees the bright side, puts the best construction on every action. What a delightful state of mind to live in! What a stimulus and benediction even to meet with it for a day! To be trusted is to be saved. And if we try to influence or elevate others, we shall soon see that success is in proportion to their belief of our belief in them. The respect of another is the first restoration of the self-respect a man has lost; our ideal of what he is becomes to him the hope and pattern of what he may become.

"Love rejoiceth not in unrighteousness, but rejoiceth with the truth." I have called this Sincerity from the words rendered in the Authorized Version by "rejoiceth in the truth." And, certainly, were this the real translation, nothing could be more just; for he who loves will love Truth not less than men. He will rejoice in the Truth—rejoice not in what he has been taught to believe; not in this church's doctrine or in that; not in this ism or in that ism; but "in the Truth." He will accept only what is real; he will strive to get at facts; he will search for Truth with a humble and unbiased mind, and cherish whatever he finds at any sacrifice. But the more literal translation of the Revised Version calls for just such a sacrifice for truth's sake here. For what Paul really meant is, as we there read, "Rejoiceth not in unrighteousness, but rejoiceth with the truth," a quality which probably no one English word—and certainly not Sincerity—adequately defines. It includes, perhaps more strictly, the self-restraint which refuses to make capital out of others' faults; the charity which delights not in exposing the weakness of others, but "covereth all things"; the sincerity of purpose which endeavors to see things as they are, and rejoices to find them better than suspicion feared or calumny denounced.

So much for the analysis of Love. Now the business of our lives is to have these things fitted into our characters. That is the supreme work to which we need to address ourselves in this world, to learn Love. Is life not full of opportunities for learning Love? Every man and woman every day has a thousand of them. The world is not a playground; it is a schoolroom. Life is not a holiday, but an education. And

THE ONE ETERNAL LESSON

for us all is how better we can love.

What makes a man a good cricketer? Practice. What makes a man a good artist, a good sculptor, a good musician? Practice. What makes a man a good linguist, a good stenographer? Practice. What makes a man a good man? Practice. Nothing else. There is nothing capricious about religion. We do not get the soul in different ways, under different laws, from those in which we get the body and the mind. If a man does not exercise his arm he develops no biceps muscle; and if a man does not exercise his soul, he acquires no muscle in his soul, no strength of character, no vigor of moral fibre, no beauty of spiritual growth. Love is not a thing of enthusiastic emotion. It is a rich, strong, manly, vigorous expression of the whole round Christian character—the Christlike nature in its fullest development. And the constituents of this great character are only to be built up by

CEASELESS PRACTICE.

The Greatest Thing in the World

What was Christ doing in the carpenter's shop? Practising. Though perfect, we read that He learned obedience, and grew in wisdom and in favor with God. Do not quarrel, therefore, with your lot in life. Do not complain of its never-ceasing cares, its petty environment, the vexations you have to stand, the small and sordid ouls you have to live and work with. Above all, do not resent temptation; do not be perplexed because it seems to thicken round you more and more, and ceases neither for effort nor for agony nor prayer. That is your practice. That is the practice which God appoints you; and it is having its work in making you patient, and humble, and generous, and unselfish, and kind, and courteous. Do not grudge the hand that is moulding the still too shapeless image within you. It is growing more beautiful, though you see it not; and every touch of temptation may add to its perfection. Therefore keep in the midst of life. Do not isolate yourself. Be among men and among things, and among troubles, and difficulties, and obstacles.

You remember Goethe's words: "Talent develops itself in solitude; character in the stream of life." Talent develops itself in solitude—the talent of prayer, of faith, of meditation, of seeing the unseen; character grows in the stream of the world's life. That chiefly is where men are to learn love.

How? Now, how? To make it easier, I have named a few of the elements of love. But these are only elements. Love itself can never be
defined. Light is a something more than the sum of its ingredients—a glowing, dazzling, tremulous ether. And love is something more than all its elements—a palpitating, quivering, sensitive, living thing. By synthesis of all the colors, men can make whiteness, they cannot make light. By synthesis of all the virtues, men can make virtue, they cannot make love. How then are we to have this transcendent living whole conveyed into our souls? We brace our wills to secure it. We try to copy those who have it. We lay down rules about it. We watch. We pray. But these things alone will not bring love into our nature. Love is an effect. And only as we fulfill the right condition can we have the effect produced. Shall I tell you what the cause is?

If you turn to the Revised Version of the First Epistle of John you find these words: "We love because He first loved us." "We love," not "We love Him." That is the way the old version has it, and it is quite wrong. "We love—because He first loved us." Look at that word "because." It is the cause of which I have spoken. "Because He first loved us," the effect follows that we love, we love Him, we love all men. We cannot help it. Because He loved us, we love, we love everybody. Our heart is slowly changed. Contemplate the love of Christ, and you will love. Stand before that mirror, reflect Christ's character, and you will be changed into the same image from tenderness to tenderness. There is no other way. You cannot love to order. You can only look at the lovely object, and fall in love with it, and grow into likeness to it. And so look at this Perfect Character, this Perfect Life. Look at

THE GREAT SACRIFICE

as He laid down Himself, all through life, and upon the Cross of Calvary; and you must love Him. And loving Him, you must become like Him. Love begets love. It is a process of induction. Put a piece of iron in the presence of an electrified body, and that piece of iron for a time becomes electrified. It is changed into a temporary magnet in the mere presence of a permanent magnet, and as long as you leave the two side by side, they are both magnets alike. Remain side by side with Him who loved us, and

GAVE HIMSELF FOR US,

and you, too, will become a permanent magnet, a permanently attractive force; and like Him you will draw all men unto you, like Him you will be drawn unto all men. That is the inevitable effect of Love. Any man who fulfills that cause must have that effect produced in him.

Try to give up the idea that religion comes to us by chance, or by mystery, or by caprice. It comes to us by natural law, or by supernatural law, for all law is Divine.

Edward Irving went to see a dying boy once, and when he entered the room he just put his hand on the sufferer's head, and said, "My boy, God loves you," and went away. The boy started from his bed, and called out to the people in the house,

"God loves me! God loves me!"

One word! It changed that boy. The sense that God loved him overpowered him, melted him down, and began the creating of a new heart in him. And that is how the love of God melts down the unlovely heart in man, and begets in him the new creature, who is patient and humble and gentle and unselfish.

The Greatest Thing in the World

And there is no other way to get it. There is no mystery about it. We love others, we love everybody, we love our enemies, because He first loved us.

The Greatest Thing in the World

The Greatest Thing in the World

III. THE DEFENCE.

Now I have a closing sentence or two to add about Paul's reason for singling out love as the supreme possession.

It is a very remarkable reason. In a single word it is this: it lasts. "Love," urges Paul, "never faileth." Then he begins again one of his marvelous lists of the great things of the day, and exposes them one by one. He runs over the things that men thought were going to last, and shows that they are all fleeting, temporary, passing away.

"Whether there be prophecies, they shall be done away." It was the mother's ambition for her boy in those days that he should become a prophet. For hundreds of years God had never spoken by means of any prophet, and at that time the prophet was greater than the king. Men waited wistfully for another messenger to come, and hung upon his lips when he appeared, as upon the very voice of God. Paul says, "Whether there be prophecies, they shall fail." The Bible is full of prophecies. One by one they have "failed"; that is, having been fulfilled, their work is finished; they have nothing more to do now in the world except to feed a devout man's faith.

Then Paul talks about tongues. That

was another thing that was greatly coveted. "Whether there be tongues, they shall cease." As we all know, many many centuries have passed since tongues have been known in this world. They have ceased. Take it in any sense you like. Take it, for illustration merely, as languages in general—a sense which was not in Paul's mind at all, and which though it cannot give us the specific lesson, will point the general truth. Consider the words in which these chapters were written—Greek. It has gone. Take the Latin—the other great tongue of those days. It ceased long ago. Look at the Indian language. It is ceasing. The language of Wales, of Ireland, of the Scottish Highlands is dying before our eyes. The most popular book in the English tongue at the present time, except the Bible, is one of Dickens' works, his Pickwick Papers. It is largely written in the language of London street-life; and experts assure us that in fifty years it will be unintelligible to the average English reader.

Then Paul goes farther, and with even greater boldness adds, "Whether there be knowledge, it shall be done away." The wisdom of the ancients, where is it? It is wholly gone. A schoolboy to-day knows more than Sir Isaac Newton knew; his knowledge has vanished away. You put yesterday's newspaper in the fire: its knowledge has vanished away. You buy the old editions of the great encyclopædias for a few cents: their knowledge has vanished away. Look how the coach has been superseded by the use of steam. Look how electricity has superseded that, and swept a hundred almost new inventions into oblivion. One of the greatest living authorities, Sir William Thompson, said in Scotland, at a meeting at which I was present, "The steam-engine is passing away." "Whether there be knowledge, it shall vanish away." At every workshop you will see, in the back yard, a heap of old iron, a few wheels, a few levers, a few cranks, broken and eaten with rust. Twenty years ago that was the pride of the city. Men flocked in from the country to see the great invention; now it is superseded, its day is done. And all the boasted science and philosophy of this day will soon be old.

In my time, in the university of Edinburgh, the greatest figure in the faculty was Sir James Simpson, the discoverer of chloroform. Recently his successor and nephew, Professor Simpson, was asked by the librarian of the University to go to the library and pick out the books on his subject (midwifery) that were no longer needed. His reply to the librarian was this:

"Take every text-book that is more than ten years old and put it down in the cellar."

Sir James Simpson was a great authority only a few years ago: men came from all parts of the earth to consult him; and almost the whole teaching of that time is consigned by the science of to-day to oblivion. And in every branch of science it is the same. "Now we know in part. We see through a glass darkly." Knowledge does not last.

Can you tell me anything that is going to last? Many things Paul did not condescend to name. He did not mention money, fortune, fame; but he picked out the great things of his time, the things the best men thought had something in them, and brushed them peremptorily aside. Paul had no charge against these things in themselves. All he said about them was that they would not last. They were great things, but not supreme things. There were things beyond them. What we are stretches past what we do, beyond what we possess. Many things that men denounce as sins are not sins; but they are temporary. And that is a favorite argument of the New Testament. John says of the world, not that it is wrong, but simply that it "passeth away." There is a great deal in the world that is delightful and beautiful; there is a great deal in it that is great and engrossing; but

IT WILL NOT LAST.

All that is in the world, the lust of the eye, the lust of the flesh, and the pride of life, are but for a little while. Love not the world therefore. Nothing that it contains is worth the life and consecration of an immortal soul. The immortal soul must give itself to something that is immortal. And the only immortal things are these: "Now abideth faith, hope, love, but the greatest of these is love."

Some think the time may come when two of these three things will also pass away—faith into sight, hope into fruition. Paul does not say so. We know but little now about the conditions of the life that is to come. But what is certain is that Love must last. God, the Eternal God, is Love. Covet, therefore, that everlasting gift, that one thing which it is certain is going to stand, that one coinage which will be current in the Universe when all the other coinages of all the nations of the world shall be useless and unhonored. You will give yourselves to many things, give yourself first to Love. Hold things in their proportion. Hold things in their proportion. Let at least the first great object of our lives be to achieve the character defended in these words, the character—and it is the character of Christ—which is built round Love.

I have said this thing is eternal. Did you ever notice how continually John associates love and faith with eternal life? I was not told when I was a boy that "God so loved the world that He gave His only-begotten Son, that whosoever believeth in Him should have everlasting life." What I was told, I remember, was, that God so loved the world that, if I trusted in Him, I was to have a thing called peace, or I was to have rest, or I was to have joy, or I was to have safety. But I had to find out for myself that whosoever trusteth in Him—that is, whosoever loveth Him, for trust is only the avenue to Love—hath

EVERLASTING LIFE.

The Gospel offers a man a life. Never offer a man a thimbleful of Gospel. Do not offer them merely joy, or merely peace, or merely rest, or merely safety; tell them how Christ came to give men a more abundant life than they have, a life abundant in love, and therefore abundant in salvation for themselves, and large in enterprise for the alleviation and redemption of the world. Then only can the Gospel take hold of the whole of a man, body, soul and spirit, and give to each part of his nature its exercise and reward. Many of the current Gospels are addressed only to a part of man's nature. They offer peace, not life; faith, not Love; justification, not regeneration. And men slip back again from such religion because it has never really held them. Their nature was not all in it. It offered no deeper and gladder life-current than the life that was lived before. Surely it stands to reason that only a fuller love can compete with the love of the world.

To love abundantly is to live abundantly, and to love forever is to live forever. Hence, eternal life is inextricably bound up with love. We want to live forever for the same reason that we want to live to-morrow. Why do we want to live to-morrow? Is it because there is some one who loves you, and whom you want to see to-morrow, and be with, and love back? There is no other reason why we should live on than that we love and are beloved. It is when a man has no one to love him that he commits suicide. So long as he has friends, those who love him and whom he loves, he will live, because to live is to love. Be it but the love of a dog, it will keep him in life; but let that go, he has no contact with life, no reason to live. He dies by his own hand.

Eternal life also is to know God, and God is love. This is Christ's own definition. Ponder it. "This is life eternal, that they might know Thee the only true God, and Jesus Christ whom Thou hast sent." Love must be eternal. It is what God is. On the last analysis, then, love is life. Love never faileth, and life never faileth, so long as there is love. That is the philosophy of what Paul is showing us; the reason why in the nature of things Love should be the supreme thing—because it is going to last; because in the nature of things it is an Eternal Life. It is a thing that we are living now, not that we get when we die; that we shall have a poor chance of getting when we die unless we are living now.

NO WORSE FATE

can befall a man in this world than to live and grow old alone, unloving and unloved. To be lost is to live in an unregenerate condition, loveless and unloved; and to be saved is to love; and he that dwelleth in love dwelleth already in God. For God is Love.

Now I have all but finished. How

many of you will join me in reading this chapter once a week for the next three months? A man did that once and it changed his whole life. Will you do it? It is for the greatest thing in the world. You might begin by reading it every day, especially the verses which describe the perfect character. "Love suffereth long, and is kind; love envieth not; love vaunteth not itself." Get these ingredients into your life. Then everything that you do is eternal. It is worth doing. It is worth giving time to. No man can become a saint in his sleep; and to fulfill the condition required demands a certain amount of prayer and meditation and time, just as improvement in any direction, bodily or mental, requires preparation and care. Address yourselves to that one thing; at any cost have this transcendent character exchanged for yours.

You will find as you look back upon your life that the moments that stand out, the moments when you have really lived, are the moments when you have done things in a spirit of love. As memory scans the past, above and beyond all the transitory pleasures of life, there leap forward those supreme hours when you have been enabled to do unnoticed kindnesses to those round about you, things too trifling to speak about, but which you feel have entered into your eternal life. I have seen almost all the beautiful things God has made; I have enjoyed almost every pleasure that He has planned for man; and yet as I look back I see standing out above all the life that has gone four or five short experiences, when the love of God reflected itself in some poor imitation, some small act of love of mine, and these seem to be the things which alone of all one's life abide. Everything else in all our lives is transitory. Every other good is visionary. But the acts of love which no man knows about, or can ever know about—they never fail.

In the Book of Matthew, where the Judgment Day is depicted for us in the imagery of One seated upon a throne and dividing the sheep from the goats, the test of a man then is not, "How have I believed?" but "How have I loved?" The test of religion, the final test of religion, is not religiousness, but Love. I say the final test of religion at that great Day is not religiousness, but Love; not what I have done, not what I have believed, not what I have achieved, but how I have discharged the common charities of life. Sins of commission in that awful indictment are not even referred to. By what we have not done, by sins of omission, we are judged. It could not be otherwise. For the withholding of love is the negation of the spirit of Christ, the proof that we never knew Him, that for us He lived in vain. It means that He suggested nothing in all our thoughts, that He inspired nothing in all our lives, that we were not once near enough to Him, to be seized with the spell of His compassion for the world. It means that—

> "I lived for myself, I thought for myself,
> For myself, and none beside—
> Just as if Jesus had never lived,
> As if He had never died."

Thank God the Christianity of today is coming nearer the world's need. Live to help that on. Thank God men know better, by a hair's breadth, what religion is, what God is, who Christ is, where Christ is. Who is Christ? He who fed the hungry, clothed the naked, visited the sick. And where is Christ? Where?—"Whoso shall receive a little child in My name receiveth Me." And who are Christ's? "Every one that loveth is born of God."

The Greatest Thing in the World

The Greatest Thing in the World

I hope you enjoyed this little book. I would like very much if you could post an honest 5-star review on Amazon or some other book site where you have an account and posting privileges. Maybe you can mention what you liked best about it.

If you found this book enjoyable, inspirational, educational or enlightening, I would hope that you tell your friends about it.

The Greatest Thing in the World

ABOUT THE AUTHOR

Bill Wylson is the author of over 50 published writings dealing with family values, religious issues and religious education. His work has appeared in *The Ensign, This People, Liberty Magazine, Success,* and others.

Bill graduated from the *Columbia School of Broadcasting* in Hollywood, CA as a commercial copywriter. He wrote trade journal ads for a major advertising agency in Los Angeles and public service announcements for a Los Angeles television station.

He has served as a volunteer Board Member of *Advocates of Single Parent Youth, Special Fun Games for the Disabled*, and on the Boards of Arts and Theater Councils. He has also served on Advisory Committees for the *Volunteer Center of Los Angeles* and on the *United Way Government Affairs Committee.*

Bill Wylson lives in Salt Lake City, Utah.

The Greatest Thing in the World

OTHER BOOKS By BILL WYLSON

Give Place in Your Heart:
31 Promises from the Book of Mormon

All of us are familiar with Moroni's promise that Christ will manifest the truth of the Book of Mormon to us by the power of the Holy Ghost. This is just one of many promises the Lord has made regarding the Book of Mormon.

In *Give Place in Your Heart*, Bill Wylson outlines 31 promises, with their attendant blessings and conditions, that the Lord would love to bestow upon you.

A New Earth
The Core Cause of Climate Change

Climate change is real.

There really should be no question about it. However, polarized views about climate issues stretch from the causes and cures for climate change to issues of trust or skepticism in climate scientists and their research.

According to NASA: "Climate change is one of the most complex issues facing us today. It involves many dimensions—science, economics, society, politics and moral and ethical questions—and is a global problem, felt on local scales, that will be around for decades and centuries to come."

The only real question is: "What can we do about it?" The answer might surprise you.

The Greatest Thing in the World

Three Minutes Eighteen Seconds:
A Prophet's Final Message to the World

Words are extremely powerful. Lord Byron poetically portrays this truth:

> "But words are things, and a small drop of ink,
> "Falling like dew, upon a thought, produces
> "That which makes thousands, perhaps millions, think."

Three Minutes Eighteen Seconds examines three "small drops of ink" that are, simultaneously, extremely powerful words spoken by President Thomas S. Monson in the April 2017 General Conference.

Hieroglyphs, Golden Plates and Typos:

On the inside cover of his first leather-bound Book of Mormon my father had written the following quotation from the prophet Joseph Smith: "I told the brethren that the Book of Mormon was the most correct of any book on earth, and the keystone of our religion, and a man would get nearer to God by abiding by its precepts, than by any other book." Directly below this quote, my father had compiled a list of scriptures which he had labeled: "Mistakes in the Book of Mormon."

Committing his writings to the future reader, Moroni candidly and apologetically acknowledged: "And if there be faults they be the faults of a man. But behold, we know no fault."

How then did my father have the boldness to make a list of mistakes in the Book of Mormon? To gain a better understanding of these 'corrections' in the Book of Mormon and how they testify to its truthfulness and authenticity, we need to understand the process involved in making plates of ore and the method for inscribing on them.

Elder Hammond and the Inspector

"You know, there's a word to describe someone who won't even bother to meet his new companion at the bus station. It starts with an 'O' or, I don't know, maybe a 'C' or something. I think it's C-a—. No, I've lost it."

Elder Hammond was a freckled-face, shy sort of bumpkin from some rural farm town in Kansas. He was awkward and withdrawn. Even in his white shirt and tie he reminded you of the type of kid you'd see in denim coveralls, wearin' a straw hat and chompin' on a thin blade of grass whilst irrigatin' the lower forty.

I knew nothing about Elder Hammond's personal life. He was just a simple, quiet, humble boy, determined and dedicated. He had no delusions of grandeur, just a desire to serve. Perhaps more than any missionary, Elder Hammond had a purity of spirit and an altruistic motivation in ministering. I pitied him. I think he actually believed he could make a difference.

The Manger on the Mantle
A Christmas Tale based on Two True Stories

The Manger on the Mantle recounts the tragic life of Mark Spencer, a man raised in a small-town who somehow becomes very lost in the massive city of Los Angeles. He didn't become geographically lost; he became spiritually lost.

As his family falls apart and his world collapses, Mark begins to realize just how tainted his life has become. He has strayed so far from the innocence of his youth and now he fears he may never find his way back.

That's when Mark meets Marvin, a sockless, root-beer-float toting ex-hippie. Together they journey the road to Bethlehem as they ponder the purpose of a birth that took place in a lowly manger.

The Manger on the Mantle is a beautiful story of hope and redemption and the joyous possibility of being given a second chance.

www.ingramcontent.com/pod-product-compliance
Lightning Source LLC
Chambersburg PA
CBHW061322040426
42444CB00011B/2740